Implementing Enterprise Observability for Success

Strategically plan and implement observability using real-life examples

Manisha Agrawal

Karun Krishnannair

BIRMINGHAM—MUMBAI

Implementing Enterprise Observability for Success

Group Product Manager: Mohd Riyan Khan

Publishing Product Manager: Niranjan Naikwadi

Senior Editor: Sayali Pingale

Technical Editor: Nithik Cheruvakodan

Copy Editor: Safis Editing

Project Manager: Ashwin Kharwa

Proofreader: Safis Editing

Indexer: Tejal Daruwale Soni

Production Designer: Alishon Mendonca

Marketing Coordinator: Agnes D'souza

First published: June 2023

Production reference: 1190523

Published by Packt Publishing Ltd.

Livery Place

35 Livery Street

Birmingham

B3 2PB, UK.

ISBN 978-1-80461-569-0

www.packtpub.com

To my mother, Asha Agrawal, for her belief in me and providing me with unconditional love and immeasurable inspiration. To my husband, Samya Maiti, for being my rock and encouraging me to stay focused regardless of the circumstances.

– Manisha Agrawal

To my father, S Krishnan Nair, for all his sacrifices, hard work, and, most importantly, unwavering commitment to his family. I lost him before I could bid a proper goodbye and this book is dedicated to him. To my mother, S Ammukutty Amma, for her unconditional love and great memories. To my wife, Sneha Mohan, for her encouragement and invaluable support. To my two angels, Tanvi and Vamika, for inspiring me and keeping my spirits high in the process.

– Karun Krishnannair

Contributors

About the authors

Manisha Agrawal is a Solution Architect with expertise in implementing scalable monitoring and observability solutions. She is committed to grooming herself and fellow women in IT to fulfill their ambitions and attain the recognition they truly merit.

As an advocate of building repeatable processes that function seamlessly at scale, Manisha possesses sharp attention to detail and a keen sense of improving existing processes. With over 12 years of experience in the finance and retail sectors, she has strong exposure to technology, people, and culture, enabling her to adapt quickly and work collaboratively toward shared goals.

Manisha holds a Bachelor of Technology in Information Technology from Rajasthan University, India, and resides with her husband in Bangalore. When she is not busy with work, Manisha enjoys indulging in her passions for traveling the world and devouring books.

Karun Krishnannair is a technology leader, analytics engineer, and architect with vast experience in working with enterprise customers and a deep understanding of monitoring and observability tools. As a technology leader and an architect, he is an avid believer in systems thinking and a strong proponent of a balanced approach to technology, tools, people, and processes to solve technology and business problems.

Karun earned a Master of Science in telecoms in 2006 and later a Graduate Diploma in Engineering Management, both from RMIT University. He has worked with two large telecommunication providers in Australia, a large financial institution, a telecommunication vendor, and two consultancies spanning over 15 years. Such a diverse background has given him the ability to see technology, people, processes, and organizational challenges from very different perspectives.

Originally from India, Karun now resides with his wife and two daughters in Melbourne, Australia.

About the reviewers

Laura Lu has over 10 years of experience in the IT industry, dedicated to observability and cloud operations. She is a former Dynatrace certified professional and delivered Dynatrace products and services to enterprise customers across APAC. She is currently employed by one of the world's largest software companies, as an observability expert. She helps the cloud operations team manage their observability services for multiple cloud products at a massive scale. She also has a focus on automation and intelligent incident detection and remediation.

I'm thankful to my former and current employers, who invested heavily in my career and personal growth, and provided the platforms for me to thrive. I also truly believe that what I have achieved today would not be possible without the support and help of all the managers and colleagues that I worked with.

Mark Helotie has worked in IT his entire adult life, with over half of that experience being in the banking and finance sectors. He has focused on the observability/monitoring arena for the last 6-7 years, with a keen interest specifically in cybersecurity. Mark has mentored many people over the years and continues to pour his efforts into the larger community to improve the tools and processes we all use every day in observability.

Table of Contents

Part 2 – Planning and Implementation

6

Gauging the Organization for Observability Implementation   67

7

Achieving and Measuring Observability Success   75

8

Identifying the Stakeholders   87

9

Deciding the Tools for Observability   97

Part 3 – Use Cases

10

Kickstarting Your Own Observability Journey   115

Preface

This book is a complete guide for technology leaders and engineers on how to scope out, plan, and implement observability in an enterprise-scale environment. The key topics covered in the book are the following:

- Observability concepts and key data formats

- Learn how to gauge the organization for implementing observability

- Principles for identifying stakeholders, tools, and processes

- Develop strategies to self-sustain the observability journey

- Case studies and guidance for setting up observability

Observability has become a popular term in the technology industry for monitoring and analytics. It's considered to be the next level of monitoring, and most vendors now offer an observability solution as part of their product suite. However, determining whether an organization requires observability, the extent to which it's needed, and the suitable skills and tools to implement it can be challenging. This book presents a systematic approach to guide organizations in developing an observability strategy. It covers the underlying principles and the logical steps for planning and executing the implementation. It also highlights the ownership of the tasks and responsibilities of different teams and how to ensure observability remains a continuous and self-sustaining process. In addition, this book introduces the Observability Maturity Model, the skills required to achieve the levels of this model, and some helpful case studies for inspiring you in your observability journey.

Who this book is for

This book is targeted toward technology leaders, architects, and initiative leads who are responsible for enhancing monitoring and/or implementing observability. The book also benefits engineers, developers, and professionals who are already working on monitoring and analytics and are responsible for scaling the observability implementation across multiple teams or at an organization.

You are expected to a have a good understanding of monitoring concepts, a general understanding of IT systems and processes, and familiarity with working with various stakeholders.

What this book covers

Chapter 1, Why Observe?, explains what observability is, what was used before observability, issues with traditional monitoring techniques, and the key benefits of observability.

Chapter 2, The Fundamentals of Observability, covers various types of data required for observability, how to map dependencies and relationships, how to handle configuration items, and KPIs used for measuring performance. When these concepts are combined, they form the building blocks for observability.

Chapter 3, The Real World and Its Challenges, presents some of the challenges that organizations may encounter while implementing observability and potential workarounds for the challenges.

Chapter 4, Collecting Data to Set Up Observability, outlines the different layers of data collection that make up the observability landscape. These layers are infrastructure, then application, business service, and organization. It also covers efficient methods for data collection across all the layers.

Chapter 5, Observability Outcomes: Dashboards, Alerts, and Incidents, discusses dashboards, alerts, and incidents in detail in the context of observability. We will look at what they mean, what the benefits are, who sets them up, who the consumer is, and how to maintain these outcomes.

Chapter 6, Gauging the Organization for Implementing Observability, is intended to encourage you to analyze the culture of your organization and find out whether it is clan, control, create, or complete culture. This will help in planning and implementing a suitable observability strategy and also helps to gauge the effort required for successful implementation. It also introduces the concept of a governance model that helps in developing and maintaining standards and frameworks for observability.

Chapter 7, Achieving and Measuring Observability Success, introduces maturity levels, namely Initial, Defined, Managed, and Quantitatively Managed, and provides guardrails to guide you through the implementation process. This chapter also emphasizes the importance of the skills required by the organization, particularly the application teams, for this cultural shift.

Chapter 8, Identifying the Stakeholders, discusses how Drivers, Users, Actors, and Supporters are the stakeholders of observability. It also provides a RASCI matrix to help you understand how all these stakeholders work together, clearly calling out their responsibilities and ownership.

Chapter 9, Deciding the Tools for Observability, provides guidance on selecting the appropriate observability toolsets for the organization, along with references to tools across different categories. You will find some guidelines on what to consider before buying, building, or leveraging observability tools.

Chapter 10, Kickstarting Your Own Observability Journey, provides ideas on what an observability implementation looks like in the real world and discusses four case studies of fictitious companies that can be used as inspiration totally or in part as suits the organization.

Download the color images

We also provide a PDF file that has color images of the screenshots and diagrams used in this book. You can download it here: `https://packt.link/EbzLW`.

Conventions used

There are a couple of text conventions used throughout this book.

Bold: Indicates a new term, an important word, or words that you see onscreen. For instance, words in menus or dialog boxes appear in **bold**. Here is an example: ""Do you need to apply **Extract**, **Transform**, **Load** (**ETL**), or filtering?"

> **Tips or important notes**
> Appear like this.

Get in touch

Feedback from our readers is always welcome.

General feedback: If you have questions about any aspect of this book, email us at `customercare@packtpub.com` and mention the book title in the subject of your message.

Errata: Although we have taken every care to ensure the accuracy of our content, mistakes do happen. If you have found a mistake in this book, we would be grateful if you would report this to us. Please visit `www.packtpub.com/support/errata` and fill in the form.

Piracy: If you come across any illegal copies of our works in any form on the internet, we would be grateful if you would provide us with the location address or website name. Please contact us at `copyright@packt.com` with a link to the material.

If you are interested in becoming an author: If there is a topic that you have expertise in and you are interested in either writing or contributing to a book, please visit `authors.packtpub.com`.

Share Your Thoughts

Once you've read *Implementing Enterprise Observability for Success*, we'd love to hear your thoughts! Scan the QR code below to go straight to the Amazon review page for this book and share your feedback.

https://packt.link/r/1-804-61569-2

Your review is important to us and the tech community and will help us make sure we're delivering excellent quality content.

Download a free PDF copy of this book

Thanks for purchasing this book!

Do you like to read on the go but are unable to carry your print books everywhere?

Is your eBook purchase not compatible with the device of your choice?

Don't worry, now with every Packt book you get a DRM-free PDF version of that book at no cost.

Read anywhere, any place, on any device. Search, copy, and paste code from your favorite technical books directly into your application.

The perks don't stop there, you can get exclusive access to discounts, newsletters, and great free content in your inbox daily

Follow these simple steps to get the benefits:

1. Scan the QR code or visit the link below

https://packt.link/free-ebook/9781804615690

2. Submit your proof of purchase
3. That's it! We'll send your free PDF and other benefits to your email directly

Part 1 – Understanding Observability in the Real World

This first part of the book provides a comprehensive guide to implementing observability in an organization. It covers various topics, including the benefits of observability, the fundamental building blocks of observability, the challenges that may arise during the implementation process, the different layers of data collection required, and the importance of dashboards, alerts, and incidents in the context of observability. The chapters provide practical guidance and tools to help readers assess their organization's culture, select the appropriate observability tools, and identify the stakeholders. Overall, this part offers a roadmap for organizations looking to implement observability and achieve greater visibility into their operations.

This part has the following chapters:

- *Chapter 1, Why Observe?*
- *Chapter 2, The Fundamentals of Observability*
- *Chapter 3, The Real World and Its Challenges*
- *Chapter 4, Collecting Data to Set Up Observability*
- *Chapter 5, Observability Outcomes: Dashboards, Alerts, and Incidents*

1
Why Observe?

Observability is a fast-growing new discipline, and all organizations want to adopt it. As you will see throughout this book, implementing observability is a journey that involves multiple teams and practices. Before you embark on this journey, it is important to understand what observability means, why it emerged, and how it can help.

This chapter will be the foundation for all the other chapters in this book. Additionally, we will introduce a fictional company that will be used throughout this book to discuss the concepts.

In a nutshell, the following topics will be covered in this chapter:

- What is observability?
- What was used before observability?
- Issues with traditional monitoring techniques
- Key benefits of observability

What is observability?

A quick Google search will give you definitions of observability in many forms from a variety of authors, vendors, and organizations. Since this book assumes you have a fair understanding of observability, we are not going to repeat a detailed definition here again. However, we will try to explain a few key concepts that are required for this book. In short, observability is not a tool, not a technology, not a strategy but a concept or a capability that will force you to think about how you are going to gain insights into the health of your application and services, at a conceptual stage of application development itself. It's a combination of robust architecture and development practices, streamlining existing data management tools, and adopting and standardizing processes that will aid the former.

In simplistic terms, many people call observability *next-generation monitoring* or *supercharged monitoring*. But it's fundamentally different in many ways. For starters, monitoring is fully dependent on a set of tools to generate the information required for operating a healthy application, while a highly observable system will generate the data that points toward existing problems or potential problems. For this to be achieved, the system developers and architects have to build observability capabilities into the product as a core function of the application itself, thereby reducing the dependency on external systems or tools to monitor. This is an ideal scenario; however, in reality, for observability, we have to depend on external applications to analyze the state of health of your applications and services. When observability is built within the application, it can reveal a lot more information about it, and as a result the dependencies on external systems or tools can be reduced significantly, as well as the cost.

Observability does not replace any application's existing monitoring tools, but it standardizes and amalgamates the capabilities of **Application Performance Monitoring** (**APM**), log and metrics management tools, and the data that's generated from applications, and effectively uses the distributed tracing methodology to achieve observability.

The Holy Grail of automation is the ability of the applications or systems to find out their issues and problems and self-heal before the users are impacted. Hence, observability can be considered a stepping stone for self-healing applications.

Throughout this book, we will use an example of a fictional company called *MK Tea* that supplies varieties of tea across the globe. They collect tea leaves from various locations, get them trucked to their plants, sort the tea as per flavors, quality, grade, package, and ship them all over the world. This entire process has many moving parts – each location where tea grows has different soil, moisture, and altitude characteristics; tea leaves, once collected, are packed and trucked to the plant by a trucking company; tea leaf sorting happens at the plant, which is an important, tedious, and manual process; tea leaves are crushed into powders of different grain sizes or dried and retained as leaves, packaged by machines, and shipped off to suppliers all over the world based on the demand for various flavors. We will see how observability can help MK Tea manage its overwhelming process, which involves human labor, skilled technicians, and fully automated machines.

You can use this example as inspiration to plan for observability in your organization.

What was used before observability?

Observability, as a term, this contradicts what you say a couple of sentences later, where you say the term was coined in 1960. please review the wording of this paragraph, with Google's definition stating "*observability is defined as a measure of how well internal states of a system can be inferred from knowledge of its external outputs.*" This started doing rounds in technical talks and presentations. This definition was coined by engineer Rudolf E. Kálmán in 1960 in his paper on control theory. In the modern IT world, observability is just a concept. Even before it became the talk of the town, some engineers were probably already building rounded monitoring systems and the ecosystem around it that made their services observable. It's just that they did not know the buzzword!

In a single instance of a web application, you can add some scripting to check the service's status, use Nagios to monitor the infrastructure, write smart logs and scrape them with scripts or some tool to keep an eye on connectivity and errors, plug results into a ticketing system such as BMC or set up SNMP traps, and there you go! The system is observable, yes that's true – all aspects of the system are covered, engineers have a hold on the infrastructure and services, they know whether the systems have connectivity, and tickets are raised when something goes wrong. It's all there. Hold on – there is something still missing though, which we will discover at the end of this section.

When thinking of what was used before observability, we are not talking about mainframe systems that were a black box for decades until some bright brains opened up that tough nut with Syncsort; there is no need to start from the beginning to understand what was used before observability. In the 90s, software and desktops were batch-oriented, had single instances, and focused less on the GUI. The outputs that they emitted were either hardware signals or code that only a few skilled technicians could decipher. With the advent of sophisticated OSs such as Linux, the game started to evolve and you might be surprised that, for a long time, humble commands such as vmstat, top, and syslogs were sought after as monitoring tools for Linux and Unix-based OSs. But we will not start from there either.

As an example, take a look at the following figure for a quick contrast between the humble beginnings of monitoring and its current state:

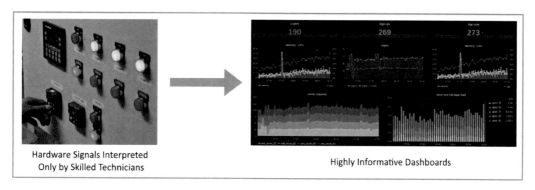

Hardware Signals Interpreted
Only by Skilled Technicians

Highly Informative Dashboards

Figure 1.1 – Monitoring then (left) and now (right) (Creative
Commons—Attribution 2.0 Generic—CC BY 2.0)

Let's fast forward a bit. The world started shrinking with the internet when the era of eCommerce started. All of a sudden, single-instance apps started evolving into monolithic apps (which we know entered the black hole soon after). And this is where we will start!

With eCommerce, infrastructure monitoring and traffic-light monitoring of services was not enough. Businesses needed frequent metrics on products, web traffic, and, most importantly, user behavior to assess current business and actionable insights to make future decisions for expansion. These came to be known as business metrics – data for the eyes of the executives. Logs being produced could no longer be at the mercy of the developers; logging frameworks and normalization techniques were introduced to help developers produce meaningful logs that could be used to derive application health and business metrics. Early-age monitoring tools such as Cacti, Nagios, scripts (shell or Python), and some commands could only cater to a handful of the monitoring requirements. Areas such as APM, customer behavior analytics, and measuring incident impact on customers remained largely untouched. As eCommerce platforms gained popularity, the volume of customers increased, and data volumes started exploding way beyond the capacity of the available monitoring tools. System architectures evolved from monolithic to distributed, making it even more difficult for traditional monitoring techniques to provide meaningful insights.

As the tech stack was increasing, each technology or tool started offering a monitoring tool. Windows had Event Viewer and SCOM, Linux had its commands, databases had RockSolid and OEM, Unix had HP products, and Apache servers had highly structured standard logs – this list can go on. Soon, the monitoring space was cluttered with micro-monitoring tools when the need was to have macro monitoring that could provide an end-to-end unified view of the distributed platforms consisting of various technologies.

As per Gartner's report, log volumes have increased 1,000 times in the last 10 years! And, all these monitoring tools and utilities have started consuming more and more data and keep evolving:

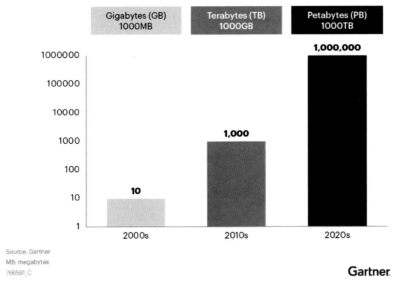

Figure 1.2 – Log volume ingestion growth (source: Gartner)

So, before observability, there was only monitoring, which was limited to a particular technology in most cases. Then, a lot of big data monitoring tools were introduced, such as AppDynamics, New Relic, Splunk, Dynatrace, and others, that could collect data from various sources and make it available to end users on a single screen. The micro-based monitoring bubbles soon started converging toward these tools and a mature ecosystem started shaping up. When you look at the fancy visualizations that these tools offer, it's hard to believe that monitoring in its primitive days was based on hardware-based signals, commands, and scripts.

Issues with traditional monitoring techniques

Traditional monitoring techniques focused on collecting and analyzing a few predefined metrics and leveraging them to analyze the system's health and use them for alerting. IT systems were managed and operated in isolation and all the IT management and engineering processes in an organization were framed around this construct and followed this isolated approach. Many IT system providers created monitoring tools to primarily monitor the application's health in isolation.

Let's discuss the issues with traditional monitoring techniques and why they no longer fit the bill for observability implementations. You may already be past these challenges, but we still recommend reading through each of the challenges as we talk about them from an observability perspective.

Modern infrastructure

Let's consider a service that depends on three applications. The traditional approach Would have identified key parameters that define the health of each of these three individual applications. Each of these services will be monitored separately, assuming that if the applications are healthy individually then the business service that depends on these applications (fully or partially) would also be healthy and will serve the customers efficiently. There was no concept of service in this approach.

This method would have worked well for a traditional infrastructure, where the application was monolithic and hosted on physical hardware in data centers. This guaranteed a certain amount of resources for the application to run. Then came virtualization, which added another layer on top of the physical hardware, and the guarantee of dedicated resources was gone. The adoption of cloud infrastructure services such as AWS and GCP and cloud-native technologies such as serverless architecture, microservices, and containers have completely de-coupled infrastructure and applications, making the IT system more complex and interdependent. These technologies have introduced a level of unpredictability in IT systems' operations. Hence the concepts, practices, and tools used for managing and maintaining the health of applications also have to change accordingly.

Pre-empting issues

One of the key issues with the traditional monitoring approach is that you pre-empt the metrics that need to be collected and monitored. Many of these key indicators or metrics are decided based on the past experiences of vendors, administrators, and system engineers. With more experience, engineers can come up with multiple and better key indicators. While this was effective to a certain extent in traditional infrastructure environments, modern distributed architecture has introduced a lot of interdependencies and complexity in IT environments, where the source of the problems or issues can drastically vary. Hence, pre-empting potential health indicators or metrics can be quite inaccurate and challenging.

Identifying why and where the problem exists

The main purpose of conventional monitoring is to detect when there is a problem. This provides a simple green, amber, or red health status indication but doesn't answer why and where the issue originates. Once the issues have been flagged, it's up to the administrators and engineers to figure out where and why the problem exists. Since modern infrastructure services are very transient, identifying the source of the problem is quite difficult or time-consuming. Hence, answering why and where as quickly as possible is critical in reducing MTTR and maintaining a stable service.

Key benefits of observability

The first step toward implementing observability is not just knowing application design, infrastructure, and business functions – it's also about considering customer behavior, the impact of incidents, application performance, adoption in the market, and the dollar value, to name a few. All members of the team need to come together to implement observability.

From the inception stage, you will require inputs from architects for design, developers for putting it together, operations for ensuring the right alert triggers, the business for clearly defining what they need, and a strategy to assess customer behavior and impact. As the project proceeds in the development and testing phases, continue to assess measures that help establish the success of a business function. Ensure that those measures are captured in outputs (logs/metrics/traces). Ensure that applications are not seen in silos but can be correlated as per business functions. This will give you visibility into business metrics and their impact on customers when things go south. The responsibility of knowing the fine-grained details of the app is shifted from architects and business analysts to every member of the team.

By now, if you have gathered that observability requires planning and hard work to implement, then you are on the right path! Congratulations, you have achieved your first milestone in your observability journey. It's not something that you think about at the end of the project so that you can tick a box before it's released into production. You need to think of observability from the inception of your new projects, plan for it and reframe the perspective for existing projects, and replan your observability strategy. We will talk about this a lot throughout this book. After all, this book has been purposely written to help you plan for observability.

The picture we have painted in this chapter is completely achievable. But what do you get after implementing observability for your applications?

- **Correlated applications that deliver higher business value**

  Modern architectures are delivered with crippling complexity, sophisticated infrastructure, smart networks, and an intertwined web of applications. A transaction originating in an on-premises web application may end up traversing containerized applications hosted in the cloud before it reaches completion. Observability lets you embrace this complexity as it focuses on correlating applications. Breaks or slowness in any application will quickly map out the impact on other applications, business functions, and customers. If your applications are observable, you will observe that the conversation in war rooms will change from bringing up the application to restoring business functions and minimizing customer impact.

- **An improved customer experience that drives customer loyalty**

  Observability delivers information faster. A high-severity incident may be super critical for infrastructure but if that particular infrastructure is only serving a very small percentage of low-value customers, it is not a high-priority incident. Observability gives you this information. It also tells you the symptoms before the customers sense them, giving you a thin window to analyze, detect, and act. Sometimes, the issues can't be fixed in this thin window, but you can still use the time to prepare your response to the customers so that social media doesn't explode and the service desk responds coherently. All your investments in observability are bound to result in improved customer experience.

- **Tools rationalization for improved ROI**

  Cut down the time required in interacting with various teams to identify the epicenter of the problem by integrating available tools that provide relevant insights for your application. Allow the tools to work in their own space but integrate the important metrics (infrastructure, application processes, deployments, database, networks, SRE, business, capacity, and more) from all the tools into a single tool that can easily construct and deconstruct your application, enabling you to measure performance on good days and manage incidents. A single or set of carefully chosen tools for observing business functions will also increase the transparency in the team as every single member of the team will have access to the same level of insights. Modern applications can generate a ton of data at high velocity. Observability helps in optimizing the data generation and collection mechanism to improve reliability and reduce cost by managing big data problems.

- **Focus on not just tech but also the process**

  To get the data you need, don't just look at writing the enterprise-grade application code. You should also invest in the process so that the problem's remediation is part of the system design. Automate all repetitive tasks along the way. It will give your team agility and reduce the room for human error. Choosing the best tool and technology will only pay off if it opens up the visibility of your system. It's not always possible to achieve 100% automation, so introduce robust practices that provide enough checkpoints to trace a problem, such as Git commits and peer reviews. Writing code can't be fully automated, but introducing Git builds a strong process around the manual task that gives end-to-end visibility into what has been deployed on the servers.

- **Data noise is converted into actionable insights**

  Correlating applications, consolidating different tools, and ingesting telemetry data can easily lead to large volumes of data, often referred to as data noise. Your observability design may be capturing thousands of parameters; what brings value is knowing which measures are central to delivering a particular business function. In observable systems, post-incident analysis is more fruitful as all the parties involved have access to information from all other teams that are involved. There is no place for playing the blame game or meddling with the information that was available only in silos earlier. Just imagine the magic observability would bring to MTTR with all its correlated systems and the involvement of different perspectives. Observable systems will allow you to take a head-on approach for the busiest days of the year as every aspect of the system is being watched and the slightest of slip-ups can be easily identified and assessed for impact. It empowers the decision-makers.

- **Foundation for a self-healing architecture**

  In a complex and interconnected IT system environment, a self-healing architecture can help in guaranteeing the service's health by quickly identifying an outage in a component or a situation that can cause an outage, and then deploying countermeasures to prevent the issue from happening or resolving the issue quickly to reduce the impact on the end customer. As you may have noticed, identifying a problem or a potential problem is a critical part of the self-healing architecture. For the self-healing actions to be effective, the detection of the problems has to be as close to real time as possible, and they must be effective and comprehensive. This is where the need for observability comes in – to be able to monitor the health of an application at the OS, application, and user experience levels.

Along with the benefits outlined in this section, observability brings many intangible benefits, such as a focus on creating service maps, strengthening CMDB, a change in the mindset of developers, and supporting people. It brings about not just a technical shift but also a cultural one. However, you can use these benefits to pitch for your observability journey. Also, keep these benefits in mind while designing observability so that you build a quality observability mechanism in the first iteration.

Summary

Now that we have come to the end of this chapter, we hope that you have a fair understanding of observability and how it differs from monitoring. Infrastructure and application monitoring has always existed in the IT landscape, but the techniques are no longer enough for modern and complex application architectures. The major drivers of this fallout are the volume and velocity of the data generated by complex and modern architectures. Therefore, observability is seen as next-generation monitoring that correlates assets, applications, businesses, and customers.

People, tools, and the organization's culture play a major role in observability implementations; we will discuss them in detail in further chapters.

2
The Fundamentals of Observability

As we go through this book, some concepts and terms will be used repeatedly, so we want to pause here and explain all the concepts that will serve as building blocks for other chapters. You may already be familiar with **logs**, **metrics**, **traces**, **service views**, **Key Performance Indicators** (**KPIs**), and **Configuration Management Databases** (**CMDBs**), but we still recommend that you read through this chapter because we are presenting these concepts with respect to observability – how they come into the picture here and who owns them.

If this is the first time you have come across any of these terms, don't worry if they don't make much sense to you on the first read. As you proceed with other chapters, your understanding of how these concepts deliver value will be enhanced. While reading through this chapter, reflect on whether your organization currently supports the concepts being discussed – if it does not, would you like to introduce them to your observability implementation?

On that note, let's get started!

Understanding logs, metrics, and traces

The foundation of observability is data! Where does this data come from? How often should you collect it? How much is too much and how much is not enough? Who is the owner of this data? Who is the keeper of this data? Who is the user of this data? Can it be ingested in its raw form? Do you need to apply **Extract, Transform, Load** (**ETL**), or filtering? Data itself is everywhere and is ever-increasing in volume with modern architectures. We will explain the forms of data that aid observability in this section and highlight some use cases for each of these forms.

The primary forms of data that we will discuss here are logs, metrics, and traces. They are often referred to as the pillars of observability. When you start your observability journey, to begin with, you may not have all three forms of data and that is alright. You can start with one or two forms and add the remaining forms to the solution as the solution matures. Having all three forms of data is nice, but it is not a prerequisite for implementing observability.

In order of increasing complexity in terms of data generation, availability, and storage are logs, metrics, and then traces. Early observability users believed that the availability of all three is mandatory for observability, but this is not true. Not all applications generate traces, metrics, or logs and not all use cases require all three forms of data, so think rationally when thinking about data formats. Let's discuss each of the forms one by one, along with their sample use cases.

Logs

Logs are the most readily available form of data and are the native form of data that has been used since the days of traditional monitoring. Logs are events in text format that can help you decode why something is wrong. Every activity in an application is logged at five standard levels – `Info`, `Debug`, `Error`, `Warn`, and `Fatal`. Keeping the use case in mind, you can carefully choose the log levels for which data will be collected. Once you have identified the data to be ingested, you need to consider the data structure – logs can be highly unstructured or perfectly structured. For example, a **Comma-Separated File** (CSV) is structured but application logs are unstructured.

How does this make a difference? The tools that you use for observability store and process the data differently based on the structure. Unstructured data is a gold mine, as it captures every detail of what transpired with the application, who the actor was, and at what time it happened. Observability tools then allow you to analyze this unstructured data and uncover the required statistics, outliers, and trends; raise alerts when an error condition is met; identify pain areas for customers while navigating through the website; monitor the health of application KPIs, the health of underlying infrastructure (servers, virtual machines, containers), request and response times, capacity saturation, and transaction rates; and identify patterns, configuration issues, and areas of poor performance in the data. This only covers a few possibilities with logs – you can add a lot more use cases based on the granularity of the data captured and the richness of the information. Logs should contain information indicating the time at which a particular activity happened in the application or the system.

Let's take a look at logs in the context of MK Tea. Various trucking companies log data as follows when they dispatch tea leaves in trucks from different locations:

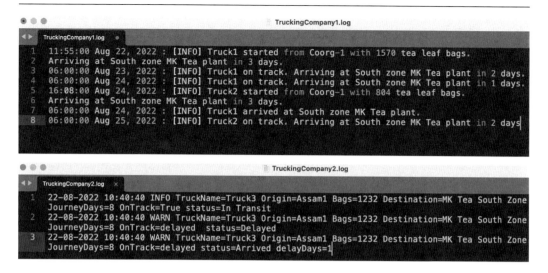

Figure 2.1 – Unstructured (top) and semi-structured log sample (bottom)

> **Important note**
> For the purpose of this discussion, the logs have obscure information.

Here are some key observations and inferences that can be made using the log data in the preceding screenshots:

- `TruckingCompany1.log` is highly unstructured and events have timestamps.

- `TruckingCompany2.log` is semi-structured, as it has key-value pairs. Fields such as `delayDays` only appear when applicable. Events have timestamps.

- The processing capacity required on a particular day can be calculated by adding up the number of tea bags that arrive on a given day.

- To keep track of the performance of the trucking companies, the number of tea bags and trucks arriving per trucking company can be plotted as a trend.

- The timestamp information in the logs can be used to keep an eye on delays in delivery and reach out to the trucking company if needed.

- Trucks from Assam are taking too long in transit, affecting the quality of the leaves. The business should consider opening a center closer to Assam in the East zone.

Now, imagine the volumes to which this log can grow as more trucking companies and their trucks are onboarded. The technique for generating the log and its structure is controlled by the application team. The observability team is only responsible for consuming this data.

With logs, always consider the storage and processing power needs of your observability setup. Since logs contain very granular information, they can be stored for a short period of time for which they remain valid for analysis. In the preceding example, it is okay to archive or delete events that are more than 15 days old. Alternatively, create data summaries or aggregate the data and store summaries for a longer time. You can also choose to filter the data before ingesting it to save processing and storage costs. All log management tools work with unstructured data in different formats; they parse the data, cleanse it, and make it available for users for analyzing and searching. The key players in this area are Splunk, **Elasticsearch, Logstash, and Kibana (ELK)**, and Sumo Logic.

Metrics

Metrics are numerical values that measure a particular aspect of the system in specific contexts called dimensions. A dimension can also be seen as a characteristic of the system. A metrics data point is made up of a numerical value, a metric name, and a few dimensions, and is collected at consistent time intervals.

Figure 2.2 – Structure of a metrics data point

Because of the precise format and structure, metrics are less taxing to store and require less processing power to analyze. Recall that `TruckingCompany1.log` and `TruckingCompany2.log` had different structures and presented similar information in different ways. Metrics are always produced in the same format across the systems involved. Bear in mind that most legacy systems do not generate metrics – however, most modern systems do, so when planning for observability, do not assume and instead ask whether metrics are available for an application. All observability tools support the collection, ingestion, processing, and analysis of metrics data points. These tools either provide built-in mechanisms via their own utilities for metrics collection or rely on `collectD` or `StatsD` running on application servers where metrics are generated.

Characteristics of metrics data

Metrics can convey a lot of information about the performance of the system, represent a snapshot in time, can be correlated easily, can be stored for longer time periods, can be summarized over time into daily or weekly aggregates to save storage, and are easy to query and use to produce excellent time-series charts for trend analysis. Metrics data does not experience bursts in volumes when user traffic rises or the system fails, but the metrics data will capture the effects of these activities – for example, higher utilization of the CPU and memory, increases in response times, connection unavailability, and so on. They are ideal candidates for triggering alerts, as the information is always precise and consistently collected.

Let's define some metrics for a tea rolling machine in our fictional company MK Tea:

RollingMachine.OperationalState

- **RollingMachine.OperationalState**: 1
- **PlantRegion**: South
- **HardwareID**: Rolling_Hardware1
- **MachineID**: MKROLL01
- **Unit**: None
- **Timestamp**: Aug 23 2022 17:05:00

The **RollingMachine.OperationalState** metric is a numerical value representing the operational state of a tea rolling machine, which can be zero or one. **OperationalState** is the name of the metric. **PlantRegion**, **HardwareID**, and **MachineID** are the dimensions for this metric. **Unit** is a field that represents the unit of the metric. In summary, we can read from this metric that the MKROLL01 tea rolling machine in the South **PlantRegion** running on Rolling_Hardware1 hardware was in an active operational state (1) on Aug 23 2022 17:05:00.

RollingMachine.TeaRolledVolume

- **RollingMachine.TeaRolledVolume**: 50
- **PlantRegion**: South
- **HardwareID**: Rolling_Hardware1
- **MachineID**: MKROLL01
- **Period**: 300
- **Unit**: KG
- **Timestamp**: Aug 23 2022 17:05:00

The **RollingMachine.TeaRolledVolume** metric is a numerical value representing the volume of tea rolled by a tea rolling machine. **TeaRolledVolume** is the name of the metric. **PlantRegion**, **HardwareID**, and **MachineID** are the dimensions for this metric. Dimensions are also known as labels. As mentioned earlier, **Unit** is a field that represents the unit of the metric – in this case, KG. The predefined metric also has another field called **Period**, which indicates the time interval at which the metric has been aggregated – in this case, 300 seconds or 5 minutes. We can read from this metric record that the MKROLL01 tea rolling machine in the South **PlantRegion** running on Rolling_Hardware1 hardware rolled 50 kilograms (KG) of tea in 5 minutes (a period of 300 seconds) when observed on Aug 23 2022 at 17:05:00.

Using an observability tool, **TeaRolledVolume** can be easily trended over time, at a granularity of five-minute intervals. The tool will also allow you to summarize data and look at hourly, daily, and weekly trends:

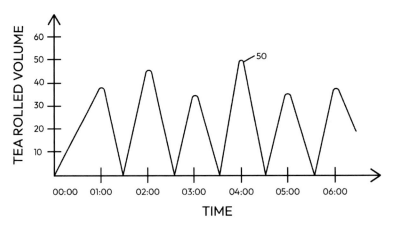

Figure 2.3 – TeaRolledVolume trend over five-minute intervals

Traces

Logs define the *what is the problem* part of the system and metrics define the *is there a problem* part. Logs and metrics have a narrow scope in an application context – they only cover specific parts of an individual system. To increase observability, we need something that can provide visibility into a request flow as it passes through multiple distributed systems. This feature is called traces, which cover the *where is the problem* part of the system. The structure of traces is like that of logs, but they are not as readily available as logs.

Challenges in generating traces

Not all applications generate traces and they are very hard to implement in legacy systems. Specific applications need to be instrumented to generate traces. Observability-tool-specific agents/collectors that can be leveraged by your application to generate trace data are available. Some open source options are also available for this purpose. Traces correlate events using a unique identifier that is correlated across various systems, which is usually not possible in legacy systems. Newer systems often use a polyglot architecture that is a combination of in-house applications and vendor-provided tools. It's very challenging to introduce a common unique identifier into these architectures. Even when the entire system is only made up of in-house applications, enabling traces is difficult, as all developers need to be in sync and conscious of the role of the common identifier when producing traces.

For example, in the following figure, **App1**, which is developed in-house, generates a record with some kind of **Unique Identifier** in **Format1**. This record then goes through **Middleware**, which generates a different **Unique Identifier** in **Format2** after processing the record received from **App1**.

Since **Format1** and **Format2** are different, there is no way to trace the record as it is generated in **App1**, traverses through **Middleware**, and reaches **App2**:

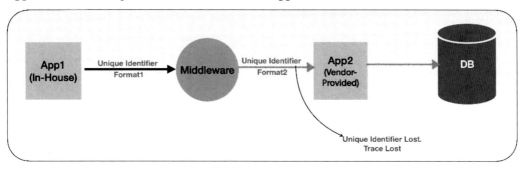

Figure 2.4 – The journey of a unique identifier

Traces look like logs but there is a subtle difference. Logs capture every activity in the system and can easily get noisy, especially at more descriptive levels such as Debug. Traces are generated at points of interaction between two separate systems to enable you to track a request path because they focus on what happened when two services or their components interacted with each other. At a high level, traces help identify the time taken at each step in the request flow. However, traces can be detailed enough to include code-level details too.

APM tools provide APIs and SDKs that can be embedded in the application code to attach a common unique identifier to requests to enable tracing. Most observability tools will allow you to capture traces for HTTP-based applications without making any code changes. This is achieved by injecting HTTP headers, producing a standard TraceID. Enabling automatic tracing is easy but it is restricted in terms of its flexibility to add more application-specific attributes. As of the time of writing, automatic tracing is very prevalent and is supported by most observability tools.

When traces are implemented in distributed architectures to track a request that spans multiple applications, it is called distributed tracing. Yes, monolithic operations can also implement tracing, which is easier and can be done via local IDEs.

A trace will contain the following:

- The name of the service
- The start time of a transaction in this service
- The end time of a transaction in this service
- Other attributes as key-value pairs – for example, parent-child response code
- The span

A complete transaction is called a trace and singular operations that make up the transaction are called spans, so it's safe to say that one or more spans make a trace.

Let's trace a sack full of tea leaves freshly plucked by a worker:

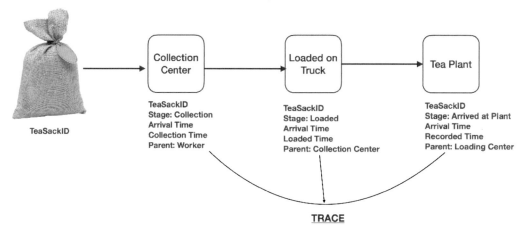

Figure 2.5 – Tracing a tea sack

Here, **TeaSackID** is the common identifier across different stages, which can be mapped to applications in the IT world. The end time and start time are part of each trace, along with some specific characteristics. Also note that a lot can transpire in each of the stages, but the trace is only being generated at touchpoints with other applications.

Now, let's take a revised look at the same example with a view of spans:

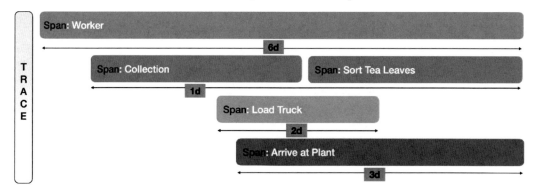

Figure 2.6 – Trace spans

Logs, metrics, and traces, when combined, are called telemetry data. Various mechanisms such as OpenTelemetry allow applications to collect telemetry in standard formats across applications and platforms. There are dedicated groups that work toward standardizing telemetry collection. This project is still maturing with time. When it reaches its full potential, collecting data required for observability will become much easier. Telemetry will be discussed in detail in *Chapter 4*.

As mentioned earlier, you don't need all three types of data from day one of your observability journey. Rather, you should focus on building an organization-wide culture that motivates you to design applications so that generating data for observability is more structured.

Along with the basic building blocks of observability – logs, metrics, and traces – other concepts such as service views, KPIs, and CMDBs are widely used in observability implementations. The next sections discuss each of them in detail.

Getting to know service views

Service views decompose applications or services into their components and/or their dependencies. They provide a true representation of the application architecture components or functions and also show how the data flows through various systems and dependencies. Service maps can act as an end-to-end blueprint of a service, which will help teams understand various touchpoints, stakeholders, and dependencies at play for any service.

Depending on the use case, there are different types of service maps, from more simple user service maps for understanding the customer experience to a more complicated technical blueprint that is used to monitor and operate a service or an application.

In general, four types of service maps are required to attain observability. Let's look at them in detail next.

User experience maps

The user experience view focuses on the end customer's experience of any service. This can be a simple measure of availability, response times, session duration, time on page, and so on for a service. This view helps developers and businesses to design and optimize services and processes to provide the best user experience to the customer by reducing lethargy, increasing ease of use, and driving or creating additional revenue generation opportunities.

Customer journey maps (processes)

A customer journey map describes the components and interactions that a consumer traverses through or experiences when consuming a service. In simple terms, it can be described as a process flow for an IT service. An efficient IT process is key to driving the efficiency of a service, enhancing the user experience, and identifying the optimum IT products or technology needed to deliver those processes as a service deliverable. These maps are used to design, plan, and build various services and subsequently operate them. To build this kind of end-to-end map depicting the interactions between various business processes for a service, all aspects of the solutions and technical (backend), non-technical (UI), and related processes need to be taken into consideration. Measures such as queue depth, request submission rates, and so on can be used to monitor the health of the customer journey.

System maps

In system maps, we will break an IT service down into its various individual components. Each of these components can be monitored individually to track the health of the IT ecosystem in which the IT service is hosted. KPIs such as CPU and memory usage, process health, runtime stats, heap size, and so on are used to monitor health. In almost all IT environments, these types of maps that monitor at the component level exist, as the traditional IT process enforces monitoring for monolithic applications as part of their operational acceptance processes.

Service aggregate maps

The preceding three service maps monitor the user experience, the underlying process that a customer has to go through to attain a certain outcome, and then the individual health of the underlying systems or applications that power the service. Now, we need a holistic end-to-end view of the service that can act as a single pane of glass, in which each sub-service is measured based on a common set of parameters to provide a simple and uniform measure to represent the overall health of the application. This will help all stakeholders, such as developer, business, product management, and various IT Ops teams, to identify, debug, and respond to events quickly and effectively. The most common metrics that can be used for this are Google's golden signals – throughput, response time, error rate, and saturation. These four metrics are very flexible and can represent all three views discussed earlier.

To create a service view, an underlying repository called a CMDB is at play, which provides information on the application and infrastructure components that make up a service. Let's discuss that next.

Exploring CMDBs

The humble CMDB as we know it is the key to all varieties of observability implementations across organizations. We will take you through what a CMDB is at a high level, why it is important in the observability context, and how your observability journey may go downhill without it.

Can you implement observability without a CMDB? Yes, you can, but it will be of lower quality and require manual intervention all the time, sometimes defeating the whole purpose of implementing observability in the first place. So, if your organization currently does not have a good-quality CMDB or it has been kept under wraps, unveil it before starting your observability journey.

What is a CMDB?

A CMDB stores metadata about a **Configuration Item** (**CI**) and the relationships between different **CIs**. As per the **IT Infrastructure Library** (**ITIL**), a CI is any component that needs to be managed in order to deliver an IT service. This information typically includes the name of the CI, the hardware being used, the software installed, the technical and business owners, the operational status, the make and model, the application to which the CI belongs, and other applications associated with it.

In our fictional company, MK Tea, a CMDB entry for a tea-drying machine will look as follows:

Attribute	Value	Description
Name (CI name)	`MKDRY01`	Name of the tea-drying machine
Business Department	`Tea Processing`	Business department to which the machine belongs
Technical Department	`Tea Drying`	Technical department to which the machine belongs
Hardware	`Tea_Machine_Platform_0.2`	Hardware on which the machine runs
Software Installed	`Tea_Machine_Software_01` `Tea_Machine_Software_02` `Tea_Machine_Software_03` `Tea_Machine_Software_04`	Software installed on the machine
Business Owned By	`Asha`	Business owner of the machine
Technical Owned By	`Neil`	Technical owner of the machine
Operational Status	`Operational`	Represents the state of the machine
Make	`2006`	Year in which this machine was made
Associations	`MKROLL01 MKSIFT01`	Upstream and downstream relationships. The tea-drying machine is related to the tea sifting and tea rolling machines
Supported By	`TEA DRYING SUPPORT`	Technical support team responsible for responding to any issues with the machine
Class	`Processing Machine`	Represents the wider category in the organization to which the CI belongs

Table 2.1 – CMDB entry for a tea-drying machine at MK Tea

Note that the preceding table is different from a database table containing the properties of the machine. A properties table will have granular details such as the make and model of the fan in the machine, the maximum and minimum possible temperature of the heater, the depth of the storage bin, the cost of purchase, and so on. This table will only contain the details that define the machine, and the properties table does not focus on how this machine can be viewed in an organizational chart of configuration items.

In an organization, a CMDB will easily contain millions of rows, one per CI. The more diverse an organization is, the bigger its CMDB will be. It needs to be updated when new configuration items are introduced or existing ones are modified. This applies to both on-premises and cloud resources. Yes, you need to have a mechanism to include your cloud resources in a CMDB.

Why is a CMDB important?

The long-standing history of service operations has proven that a CMDB is helpful for various ITIL processes, such as incident management, change management, problem management, capacity planning, and cost planning. Let's explore how it helps in observability.

The CMDB is the repository that maintains relationships between CIs. This means that when a particular CI is impacted, the IT team can look at the CMDB and identify which other CIs and related technical and business services may also be impacted or can be expected to run at a degraded level. Observability also focuses on the relationships between services and thus leverages CMDBs heavily. The quality of the CMDB has a tight relationship with the quality of observability.

A CMDB also highlights the critical CIs. For example, a particular CI that has a relationship with multiple other CIs and services is highly critical, as any impact on it will eventually cascade to the related CIs, increasing the magnitude of the impact. While designing observability, you can provide higher weightage to the KPIs that govern the health of the critical CI. (Note: KPIs will be discussed in the next section.)

In *Chapter 5* of this book, we will discuss alerts. Identifying the right support team that is responsible for responding to any issues in the CI is a must for raising a meaningful alert. This mapping is also provided by a CMDB. It leads to faster resolution of the problem.

Establishing relationships between the CIs leads to building service maps, which have been discussed in the preceding section, *Getting to know service views*. A CMDB is also an auditor's delight. A lot of compliance and audit-related information such as the view of the infrastructure, the software installed, and the hardware being used is readily available in a CMDB. Therefore, if your observability implementation also includes compliance (at an advanced stage), the CMDB is an important enabler.

Automation is an important aspect of observability and it is bound to fail if CIs need to be fed manually. Any automation capability for upgrading a software component as soon as an upgrade is available should be able to connect to the CMDB to get the latest map of CIs for an application and run the upgrade without human intervention.

CMDB providers and their life cycles

A CMDB is typically built using discovery processes and data imported from other tools. Discovery processes scan the entire IT landscape for hardware and software details. CI details can also be imported from **IT Finance Management** (**ITFM**) tools and **Software Asset Management** (**SAM**) tools. Further details on discovery processes and ITFM and SAM tools are beyond the scope of this book. A reliable and robust CMDB will use automation, limiting manual intervention only to CIs that cannot be discovered via automation. This is part of the **IT Service Management** (**ITSM**) processes and is managed by the ITSM team right from discovery to providing mechanisms for other tools to integrate. Observability tools consume CMDB data via accessing the database or API calls. All common ITSM systems, such as Service Desk, ServiceNow, IBM Tivoli, Zendesk, and Micro Focus, provide CMDB implementations. Choose a CMDB tool based on the use cases in your organization and the potential consumers of the data. If your organization has a CMDB, work on evaluating its quality and figure out the best possible way to consume the data in your observability implementation. It takes a lot of effort to build and maintain a CMDB, but it's all a waste if no one is consuming it. Don't forget to thank your ITSM team for maintaining the beast. This *single source of truth* can easily become misleading if not updated regularly for both on-premises and cloud CIs, so speak to your ITSM team to understand the coverage of CIs and update schedules in detail.

A lot of our discussions in the book will refer to CMDBs directly or between the lines. They play a major role in assessing the impact of issues, identifying critical services, and powering automation.

> **Important note**
> A CMDB has many intrinsic details around discovery; defining classes; refreshing and updating data; exposing APIs, dashboards, and reports; and so on. This section only looks at the CMDB from an observability point of view and does not aim to discuss CMDBs in further detail.

Identifying KPIs

As discussed in earlier sections of this chapter, to build a service view, we have logs, metrics, traces, service maps, and, lastly, a CMDB that holds all these components and relationships between them. Let's start measuring the performance of each component. In generic terms, we can call them **Key Performance Indicators** (**KPIs**).

A KPI defines the measures or factors that need to be monitored to track the health of a system or a performance indicator that the organization strives to achieve or meet. Once a service has been defined and the dependencies have been identified and mapped, KPIs are used to keep track of the performance of these individual components and dependencies, which reflects the overall success of the service.

KPIs are quantifiable measurements used for the following:

- Providing a quick high-level view of the service health
- Defining key indicators that can affect the service health
- Quickly identifying areas that need attention
- Measuring business impact

Let's try to take a real-life example of an e-commerce business and apply it to various service maps:

- **User experience maps**: User experience KPIs express how a user interacts with a website and uses its features and services. When designing these websites, metrics related to the user experience can be configured to be collected continuously and automatically and can be built into the process or derived from the workflow. The task completion rate, execution time, navigation time, error rate, and customer satisfaction reviews can be used to effectively gauge the user experience.

- **Customer journey maps**: In the case of an e-commerce website, the normal workflow is that the customer searches for a product, reads the description, compares other similar products, reads reviews of products and the seller, and then finally decides to buy something. Once the decision has been made, the product is added to the cart, the delivery location is added, and, finally, the payment is made. There will be an option to cancel the order and return faulty products as well. In each of these workflow steps, KPIs such as search versus navigation, search versus buy, time to delivery, product cancellation rate, product return rates, and so on can be used to identify the efficiency of each stage of the workflow and the overall business process.

- **System maps**: The underlying technology used for a typical e-commerce website includes a website, a database that stores the information of the products, an authentication system to validate the customer, an **Enterprise Resource Planning (ERP)** system to take care of orders and deliveries, an AI engine for product recommendations, a payment gateway to make payments, and so on. Each of these components can have a list of KPIs that represents its health. These KPIs can be framed after consulting the relevant subject matter experts – for example, a database administrator can come up with KPIs related to databases, and similarly, ERP systems, web servers, payment gateways, and so on can have their own sets of selected KPIs. The idea is to overlay the health of each component over the system maps to see the health of an entire fleet.

- **Service aggregate maps**: The difference between service aggregate maps and system maps is that service aggregate maps don't care about the health of individual components. As long as the services that each component provides are healthy, the service aggregate maps show the service as healthy. Modern IT applications are architected with resiliency and **High Availability (HA)** in mind – applications can be run in HA mode, can be containerized to be spun up and down as required, and so on. Now, taking the example of the e-commerce website, several web servers may be hosting the website. If any of the web servers are faulty, the web server IT support team needs to know how to investigate, do root cause analysis of, and remediate the issue. However, a service manager does not care about this until the customers are impacted. In simple terms, service aggregate maps are for service managers who are interested in the end-to-end health of the service and the system maps for all four IT support or operation teams.

In practice, identifying KPIs to be monitored requires several iterations between observability experts and application/service SMEs. This is a daunting task – the first draft of KPIs will keep evolving over time until it reaches the final stage. As a starter, Google has suggested four standard KPIs that broadly apply to all types of applications and services. These standard KPIs are known as Google's golden signals. When you identify the specific KPIs for your services and applications, you can start by setting up the golden signals. Let's explore golden signals in the next section.

Google's golden signals

For service aggregate maps, four **golden signals** can be used as KPIs for monitoring the health of the overall service and the interface between various components without looking at the underlying infrastructure. This is one of the most commonly used KPIs for an aggregate view, as these KPIs are very generic and very flexible, so they can be applied to multiple scenarios. Almost all the issues that a service can have will be reflected by any one of these four signals. Let's look at them in the context of an e-commerce website:

- **Latency**: As mentioned previously, for any commerce website, many IT services such as databases, ERP systems, web servers, recommendation engines, and so on interact with each other to fulfill an e-commerce workflow. The latency of these interactions is a good indicator of how much time it takes to complete a request. If the database is slow to respond to requests, this will be reflected in the latency metrics of the database. Similarly, if the web services are slow or have a critical backend error, this, again, will be reflected in the latency of the web servers.

- **Throughput**: Throughput measures the amount of traffic between two components of the service for a system to effectively work – at a given point in time, a specified amount of traffic has to move. By monitoring this traffic, we can gauge the performance of the service. For example, if there is a slow database issue, the customer interaction will be slow and this will be reflected in the throughput numbers of the web servers and also in the number of database requests. Throughput can be a technical measure of the number of HTTP requests, the number of database connections, and so on, or it can be a business measure such as the number of purchases or the number of product searches.

- **Errors**: The rate of failures that happen in each of the components is a reflection of a health issue. The failures can be direct failures within the application stack or can be instigated by external environments such as networks, storage, and DNS servers that impact the health of a technical interface. A sudden increase in error rates in any of the components can easily be monitored and can be a quick pointer toward the potential source of a problem. For each of the interfaces, errors can vary based on the underlying technology – for example, HTTP 500 server errors, 400 client errors, database connection errors, deadlock errors, and so on.

- **Saturation**: Saturation can represent how constrained your services are running in relation to the capacity of each interface. In simple words, it shows the utilization of each interface. Going back to the example of an e-commerce website, each of the components is built with a certain amount of capacity and throughput in mind – hence, each of these interfaces is also configured to handle a certain amount of load. A metric that shows how much of this capacity has been utilized is a powerful metric for understanding how a service can handle different types of traffic volumes and when a system will start to degrade in performance.

KPIs play a crucial role in helping teams understand how their systems are performing and identify areas for improvement. We have provided guidelines on identifying KPIs and have also shared some common KPIs that are quickly becoming industry standards. You can leverage this information to build your own KPIs, but always remember that over time, as applications mature, you may need to add new KPIs or factor in more calculations into the existing ones.

Summary

To conclude, in this chapter, we learned about the different types of data required for observability; understood how to map dependencies and relationships; learned how to handle the configuration items; and, finally, learned about the KPIs used for measuring performance. When all these concepts are combined, they form the building blocks for observability.

3

The Real World
and Its Challenges

Observability as a concept is a no-brainer, a capability that helps in increasing the stability of services, improves reliability, helps developers to build better products, helps designers design more user-friendly services, helps in automation, and so on. Who doesn't want such a capability?

The issue is that observability is not just about buying and installing a few sets of tools. It is about driving the adoption of observability concepts and tools, empowering the whole organization to follow a data-driven decision-making culture, ensuring that success is measured and improvements are tracked, shared, and celebrated, and most importantly, showing the value on a continuous basis to ensure sustained funding for the initiative.

For the successful implementation of any large initiatives that span across an organization, it's very important to understand the environment, the culture, the people, and the technology stack of the organization, and observability implementation is no different. A lack of consideration for any of these factors can be detrimental to success. This chapter elaborates on some of the key real-world challenges and potential solutions.

Is observability difficult to implement?

As this book is on how to implement observability in a large organization, the answer to the question *Is observability difficult to implement?* is yes, it is difficult to implement at scale. Any project that any organization undertakes will have a set of key parameters for success, a set budget, a set of skills required, and a set time frame. When the key success parameters vary in complexity and scale, a set budget is difficult to define and the level of skill required is diverse. Most importantly, the time frames are difficult to set. Then you will end up with a very difficult project to implement.

As mentioned earlier in the book, observability is a concept that requires changes in how an organization designs, develops, and operates application services. It may sometimes involve changing the culture within the organization, and you can be sure that that is quite a challenging task. There are many examples where organizations came back from the verge of bankruptcy by rediscovering and reinventing themselves – such as Apple. Apple had to make a few difficult decisions to achieve this, shut down a few products that didn't make any money, let go of a few things, reprioritize goals, and reorganize itself, changing the way it operated. That paid off handsomely and ultimately created a technology behemoth. The changes that Apple made were done out of necessity for survival, and observability is the same.

We have mentioned the story of Apple here not to scare everyone, but just to illustrate that for observability to be implemented in a large organization, it needs a tectonic shift in thinking and behavior in the organization. Organizations should be ready to understand and accept that the architecture and landscape have changed significantly, and traditional IT practices no longer meet the requirements. Hence, they need a full ground-up review of practices, skills, organizational structure, and tools. All these changes in people, processes, and tools must be synchronized to get the optimum outcome.

Let's take the example of an e-commerce company. From a technical landscape perspective, to deliver its services, the organization has to use a mix of technologies that are either developed in-house or bought off the shelf, and also use services from other **Software as a Service (SaaS)** platforms. The whole technical solution has to be capable of coordinating all the activities of the internal as well as the external stakeholders to provide an end-to-end service. Now, to provide observability, across the breadth of the services, a common framework that includes software standards, a set of carefully chosen observability tools, a set of common data structures, and so on needs to be endorsed at the architecture level and implemented during procurement and development, and at the operational level. For an organization that already has an existing service and an associated technical solution is available, the transition has to be made, one step at a time, as per the common framework.

Let's take some common patterns of challenges that you may encounter while implementing observability at scale.

Google versus a financial institution

In simplistic terms, Google develops its applications and standards in-house and a financial institution buys software and technologies and integrates them to provide a service. Since Google builds solutions from the ground up, the opportunity to implement observability at all stages and levels of it's own technology stack is higher compared to the financial institution that depends on Google and multiple other vendors to implement observability. Hence the scope, plans, and timelines for observability implementation in these two organizations will be different.

Diverse service versus focused service

Some organizations – let's say a financial institution – provide a diverse set of services that requires diverse technical and business solutions. The technology inventory, business processes, customer journeys, aggregate maps, and so on will be very diverse. Compared to this, a taxi service company provides one or two services at a massive scale, where thousands of customers must be served around the globe for a single service. Here also, the approach will have to be different, as the diversity of the services can make the maps more complex and create more dependencies between services. Making the services observable in a small organization with a diverse portfolio can be as hard as making the services observable in a large organization with a few services.

Technology leader versus follower

Organizations that are working on the cutting edge could lead the industry with innovation, by quickly adopting new techniques and practices, compared to an organization that is risk averse and follows industry best practices. Implementing observability in a technology-leading organization can be relatively easy as these organizations are typically very agile and receptive to new concepts and out-of-the-box ideas.

In summary, implementing observability is like changing the way an organization thinks and lives. Each organization's characteristics, ways of working, diversity of services on offer, and so on will all contribute to the complexity and all these factors need to be holistically considered for the implementation.

We will discuss organization cultures in detail in *Chapter 6* of this book.

Challenges faced by organizations in the real world

We discussed the benefits of observability in *Chapter 1*, where we talked about correlation, improved customer experience, the rationalization of tools, improved processes and technology, actionable insights, and how observability drives automation. To realize all these benefits, a solid implementation is needed, which has its own challenges. Let us take you through some key challenges that everyone faces when planning observability in their organizations. These are the most common and logical challenges for which you should prepare in advance.

Infrastructure and architecture complexity

With modern architectures, infrastructure is no longer limited to on-premises. It consists of applications entirely or in part hosted on public and private clouds, containerized platforms, microservices, and of course on-premises servers. This complicated web of sophisticated infrastructure pieces generates high-velocity data that can quickly scale up to petabytes of ingestion per day. Most organizations are doing hundreds of terabytes of ingestion into their observability tool set on a daily basis. Considering these data volumes, finding useful information and reacting to it in near real time poses a great challenge in terms of correlating the data. In complex polyglot architectures, to make the services observable, correlation is essential and should be done quickly. Furthermore, no two datasets look alike, and correlating them to produce meaningful business information is an engineering marvel and an exhausting exercise without using observability tools. It's not just data collection that is challenging; data storage and efficient retrieval are even bigger challenges. You will need to clearly plan out how much and from where you will ingest data, where you will store it, and for how long. Stepping down from infrastructure into the architecture realm, you may encounter some other challenges, such as application silos, too many data sources, instrumenting legacy applications, data filtering, aggregation and routing, and most importantly, identifying the right sources of data across layers. You will need to build or design a user interface that allows users to analyze and troubleshoot the data being collected. With so many moving pieces in infrastructure and architecture, it is much easier said than done!

Mindset and culture

Terms such as DevOps, SRE, and observability have gained popularity in the past decade. IT operations teams, developers, project management, and organizations as a whole have undergone a lot of transformation in how they operate, build, and deliver at scale. The adoption of a new discipline is not limited to technology; a major portion of the success comes from the people who use the technology and the culture of the organization. The most common pain point in this area is the *build-and-forget* culture. Great tools for observability can be acquired or built and a process is also created around them, but if the tools and the process are not revised frequently by the people, the tools will end up losing their worth. Organizations where monitoring and observability are an afterthought are severely plagued by a lack of the right skill set to propagate and maintain observability tools and processes. Users of the tools start seeing the onboarding of their application onto observability tools as an additional piece of work, a mere step toward being compliant. This is a major cultural issue.

Outsourcing the building of observability solutions with no skill set within the organization to further enhance and support the solution is set for doom. Hiring for observability talent is tedious as it's a very new discipline and there are very few skilled professionals in the market. People and culture are intrinsic to the success of observability implementation as it requires constant participation and evolution from the users and the keepers. We understand that you definitely cannot change your organization's culture overnight but keep it in mind while planning your observability journey. All tools (vendor-acquired or built in-house) have great functionalities. You need to find the ones that are in perfect tune with your organization.

A lack of executive support

Today, executives are under immense pressure to keep up with emerging trends in their fields and steer the organization forward. They must keep up with the cloud, data analysis, operations, and infrastructures. Only with a bird's-eye understanding of all these areas can they carve out a good observability strategy for their organization because all these areas operate in tandem, and advances or setbacks in one have impacts on the others.

For example, Kubernetes created an upheaval in infrastructure, analysis, and operations. Required skill sets had to be realigned, projects had to be redesigned, and budget definition had to be revised. Executives need to support all these areas; otherwise, the organization's growth will be impacted. The adoption of a discipline or tool largely depends on how executives promote it in their charters. They will usually discuss the benefits and make time in existing task queues to explore and implement the shifted priorities. They are responsible for bringing in compliance and governance policies that help in measuring the success of these implementations. Something disruptive like observability also requires a shift in mindset and unless executives are totally convinced of the idea, they will not be able to derive the shift in their people's mindset.

You will often see that a particular tool does well in one organization and fails badly in another even when both organizations are in the same domain. Support from executives is one of the major drivers in this case. While planning your observability journey, you need to ensure that your executives are in favor of the proposed strategy. It can get challenging in the constructs of power and influence.

Tools galore

It is very common for an organization to have 20+ monitoring tools. There are always some licensed tools and corresponding open source variants in the mix. It is no surprise to see multiple tools for the same function, for example, infrastructure monitoring. The reason for having multiple tools is twofold – one, tools have been acquired over time but not decommissioned as more advanced tools become available in the market; two, teams are working in silos and acquiring their own stack of tools.

The problem with having too many tools means having too many agents that run on the application servers, all demanding a share of the resources, however small. And, there is always overlap in the data that the tools collect. Finding the needle in this haystack becomes even more difficult. If you can relate to this problem, you are not alone!

Today, vendors are putting their best sales propositions and organizations with money end up buying multiple tools. There is also a conflict among users of these tools. You will often see that IT operations and developers have different levels of access to the same tool being used for managing an application. This causes a mindset problem. The teams think that the tool is for the people on the other side, leading to severe underuse of the tool's capabilities.

Mechanisms to measure success

You can build a world-class product that delivers but you cannot really drive interest and adoption unless you have some metrics to show how it's helping customers. Measuring success becomes a challenge later if not planned properly while designing the observability solution.

You will need to weave in mechanisms to help you measure success factors such as **Mean Time to Detect (MTTD)**, **Mean Time to Recovery (MTTR)**, and **Service-Level Agreements (SLAs)**. Keep a stocktake of the current incident landscape for application services and measure it against the emerging landscape after observability implementation. If your organization operates in the SRE model, you should closely monitor the error budget and time to market. If your organization measures success on some other specific KPI as well, ensure that your solution captures that as well.

The price tag

Organizations define innovation and spending budgets that are allocated to different departments. Observability needs to cover the infrastructure, application, business and customer experience. This requires tools, time, effort, and human resources to develop and maintain the whole observability implementation. Tools are costly and skilled human resources to maintain them are expensive and difficult to find. Hardware has to be procured for collecting data, processing, and analyzing it. Buying tools and hiring the right people will give you the technology and skills, but educating users to adopt the solution is another uphill battle. You have to take calculated steps while using the budget. If you spend too little, the solution will be limited in its capabilities and you may not be able to reap any benefits; if you spend too much, what if the solution is not well adopted by users. Today, organizations need to deliver at speed and fail fast, all while maintaining productivity. This applies to observability as well and can only be achieved with solid foundations built on automation and modern technologies, which cost considerable money, time, and effort.

As applications are moving toward multi-cloud architectures, observability is finding its feet very fast. It's a game of volume, velocity, and a variety of data. Observability definitely has its benefits, but the road to achieving it is not easy or smooth. It demands constant evolution as the IT landscape and business functions change. We hope that the challenges highlighted here will help you in planning observability for the success of your organization.

Overcoming challenges

We don't want to leave you wondering how to work through the challenges listed in the previous section. So, we will introduce you to some solutions that you can use as inspiration to tailor a solution for your organization. Let's take a look at some of the generic solutions to observability challenges.

Navigating through infrastructure and architectural complexity

Do not go for a 100% coverage approach. Ingesting every bit and fragment of available data in all forms is not going to give you meaningful information. Like cloud-native start-ups that have observability in mind from day one, during the application implementation stage, decide on the data points for each touch point. Have discussions with the architects and developers to identify the logs, metrics, or traces that will be ingested into the observability platform. Any form of data can be chosen as long as it provides the required information.

For components that are to be planned in the future, look for extensibility options in your current data format choices. For example, if you choose metrics for an existing component, place a requirement with the developers that the new components should also be able to emit metrics for connecting the services in an end-to-end transaction flow.

Planning the sources of data well ahead will help you plan the storage as well, and set up policies for retrieval and access on your observability platform. Always remind yourself that a successful observability implementation is nurtured over time not plugged in at the end.

Taking stock of your estate

People and culture cannot be changed overnight just for observability implementations, so take stock of what you have and work your way around it. If your organization is good at implementing processes and adapting to change, you can expect good participation from the users to keep your observability implementation alive and evolving. Otherwise, plan for implementation in baby steps, measure the response, and then proceed.

Guidelines on measuring success have been discussed in *Chapter 7* of this book.

Focus on building capabilities within the team rather than hiring an all new team. People who have been part of the organization can drive change from within. New people come with their own baggage and take time to adapt to the new normal. For a successful implementation, more than the observability team, it is the application teams who need to embrace the shift and work hand in hand to extract maximum value from the implementation.

If you are not in a technology-centered organization, plan for user education sessions on how observability can make life easier and how application teams can participate in the journey. Create a need for observability, show the value, and then sell it. Once teams see the value, they will participate in evolving the implementation. Do not settle till you reach a culture that promotes a proactive understanding of the issues and thought process to optimize it.

How can executives help?

Executives play a major role in increasing the visibility of observability implementations. They spread the word about the offering and the benefits to be gained out of it. Talk to your executives not just for funding to onboard the right tools and people; also talk to them about the upcoming organization-wide initiatives where observability can help. If you are an executive yourself, focus on making the right training and technology playgrounds available for your teams so that they can know what is possible and how to build in the context of the organization. Allow your teams the space and time to act upon ideas.

Executives may not have the deepest insight, but they will have the broadest reach both in terms of knowledge and influence. As an observability team, you need to work directly with your executives as the implementation is going to be a major mindset shift, a money burner, and dependent on adoption by application and platform teams. Unless such a change is driven from the top, it will not be successful.

Tool rationalization and usage

As discussed earlier, in a large organization, there might be a large inventory of tools that have been acquired and are being used for various use cases. These individual tools can create an island of data within the organization and in most cases, sharing this data is nearly impossible. As discussed in previous chapters, for a successful implementation of observability, we need data from different levels of the technology stack, that is, infrastructure, application, business service, and so on. To achieve this, the collection/generation, transportation, and processing of data have to be streamlined and standardized. Collecting once, sharing, and using multiple times should be the underlying principle. Standardization will result in reduced cost of their operation and ensure consistency of data across the organization. It also has to be noted that the tools selected after rationalization and consolidation can only satisfy the majority of use cases; there will always be a need for specialized tools for a specific purpose. The intention behind this rationalization is only to achieve as much consistency as possible and avoid data islands.

For selecting the tools, refer to *Chapter 9* of this book, where this is discussed in great detail. There are many tools from many vendors available on the market, and decision-makers will be spoilt for choice. The two key selection criteria should be the compatibility of the tools with the technology stack that the organization has and the ability of the tools to work with each other, especially for sharing data.

What does success look like?

This is one of the questions that has been repeatedly asked in all organizations during planning and implementation, not just of observability, but also even for an enhanced monitoring solution. When an application starts the journey from traditional monitoring and alerting maturity to an enhanced monitoring capability, and then finally to a highly observable system, the criteria for success will vary at each stage.

Guidelines on measuring success have been discussed in detail in *Chapter 7* of this book.

Let's take an example of an application that has a very traditional infrastructure and application monitoring solutions. Most of the time, success is measured using MTTD, MTTR, or SLAs. When the monitoring capability has been enhanced using a log analytics tool or using an APM, you can easily see a vast improvement in these metrics. Log analytics and APM tools are purpose-built to help operations teams to detect issues early and help in repairing them quickly, thereby reducing the impact on the end consumer. Therefore, after implementing the log analytics and APM tools, there is less room for improvement of the metrics used for measuring success as the tools, by default, bring a lot of stability into the existing components and prepare the ground for monitoring and enhancing the stability of future enhancements. Please remember the end goal for attaining observability is not just to improve detection and early repairing of issues but also to improve the user experience and correlation capabilities, close the loop by learning about and improving services, self-healing opportunities, and so on. Hence, the success criteria should be based on these metrics for the advanced stage of observability. The number of users of the observability stack, the user experience score, the process simplification/improvements made, actionable alerts versus false positives, service health metrics, user acquisition/retention rate, and so on can be some of the criteria used in the advanced stage.

Cost rationalization

Justifying the cost and showing **Return on Investment** (**ROI**) is the most important part of any initiative within an organization and for its long-term success. As we have discussed before, observability is about changing the culture within the organization and most of these initiatives will span multiple years. Hence, showing the value and ROI continuously is critical for gaining the support of the senior executives and sponsors and for sustained funding.

The planning and implementation of observability provide an opportunity for organizations to rationalize their tools and thereby reduce the number of tools that have been used in the organization, which can result in significant cost savings. In the initial stages, along with the improvement in MTTR, MTTD, and operational stability, these cost savings can be an added benefit. Once the investments in chosen tools and processes are made in the initial stages of the observability journey, further success depends on how the organization adopts those tools and standards, and implements and maintains them in their respective areas. In the next stages (after initial setup), the costs are mainly related to development, enhancements, adoption, and operations.

By introducing a robust reporting mechanism using key metrics that we have discussed in the preceding section and in *Chapter 7*, the benefits of the advanced stages of observability can be measured, tracked, and reported and can be used to justify these additional costs. Most of the time, these measures cannot be framed for the whole organization but for very targeted projects and/or initiatives. The main challenge will be to record, track, and report the success stories (however small they may be) across the organization and the benefits it brings to the organization as a whole.

The solutions that we have proposed are generic and may or may not apply to your organization as is. You can definitely use them as guiding principles to work through the challenges discussed earlier. Observability implementations are successful when there is good participation from application teams and executives. Do not follow a trend but think of what works best for your organization and then plan.

Summary

Observability is exciting as it has all the right elements for spearheading success. It involves automation, scale, proactiveness, efficient operations, visibility of complex applications, and improved customer experience. However, it is good to be aware of the on-the-ground challenges before getting swayed by the winds of change.

We presented to you the challenges that you may face and some workarounds. You will definitely have your own challenges and limitations, but we hope that this chapter will help you overcome them. Since observability is a fairly new discipline, you may not get all the help you need from external sources. So, start steady and in small steps so that you have an opportunity to correct yourself, building a robust foundation along the way.

4

Collecting Data to Set Up Observability

Observability comes to life with data. It's the data that provides the insights, lets you analyze, make meaningful decisions, act in time to save service degradation, and in many cases, save your customers and your rapport with them. So, in your observability journey, carefully plan for what data you will ingest, from where, and at what frequency.

In *Chapter 2*, we talked about types of data – logs, metrics, and traces. This chapter leverages that knowledge and introduces you to the layers in the application architecture at which data is to be collected in one of these three forms. We have chosen four layers for this book – **infrastructure**, **application**, **business service**, and **organization**. Please note that these may or may not apply to your application architecture, and that is absolutely fine. We have chosen broad layers that will apply in general to most application architectures.

Data collection layer one – Infrastructure

Infrastructure is the atomic layer in any architecture on which the whole stack of applications runs, serves customers, and drives revenues. Whether or not your team or organization is responsible for managing the infrastructure, having a view of the state of infrastructure in an observability implementation helps to quickly isolate or rule out infrastructure-related problems. This discipline that focuses on collecting health, resource utilization, and performance data of the infrastructure is called **IT Infrastructure Monitoring (ITIM)**.

In this section, we will discuss what infrastructure means in the IT world, how we can collect data to monitor it, and why you should bother monitoring infrastructure at all.

Understanding infrastructure

In modern complex application architectures, infrastructure components can include (but is not limited to) physical servers, virtual machines, databases, containers, appliances, networks, storage devices, and other backend components. Some common interfaces are API calls, which may either be made directly to the database or be agent-based; this can be done using both proprietary and open source tools. Therefore, data collection mechanisms and tools are also different. While these components may be related in some cases, such as virtual machines running on top of a physical host, they run largely independent of each other in terms of operation. This makes data collection less complicated.

All the IT infrastructure co-exists to support your application requirements. A fault in one will impact the other components, support teams, and customers as the load increases on them. In some cases, faults can also lead to underutilization as traffic to those components can be cut off.

Collecting data to monitor infrastructure

Infrastructure monitoring refers to the performance and health monitoring of the hardware and the operating system. In some servers, there can also be a virtual machine that sits on the hardware. Here is a graphical representation of typical server components with regard to infrastructure monitoring:

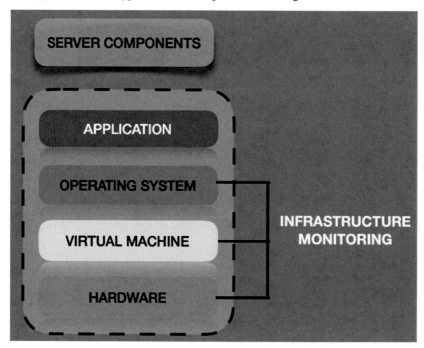

Figure 4.1 – Typical components of an IT infrastructure

Commonly, infrastructure health data consists of measurements of the **central processing unit** (**CPU**), memory, disk, and network utilization. It can be extended to keeping a tab on swap, open file descriptors, **input/output operations per second** (**IOPS**), electricity usage, hard drive status, fan temperature, and more. Infrastructure monitoring tools allow you to trend on the data, quickly highlighting overutilization or underutilization of the resources. Keep in mind that even in the virtual world, these resources are only finite, and it is important to keep a tab on them. Spikes in CPU or memory utilization often indicate unexpected heavy load or hardware faults. If the disk is full, it can lead to the shutting down of the application services.

Infrastructure data is a time series and can be in the form of logs or metrics but never in the form of traces. Metrics are a preferred format as the structure of this data is standard per infrastructure component and can be collected at a fixed frequency given that the chosen frequency is equal to or higher than the frequency at which data is generated.

The typical method of collecting infrastructure data is via **agent** installation on the infrastructure component. This agent is then tuned to pick up the required data at a fixed frequency. Some tools will also allow you to control data collection frequency at per host level. The agent then ships the data to the monitoring platform for analysis, visualization, and storage. Agent-based infrastructure data collection can be easily automated by configuring the monitoring tool accordingly. One of the best practices in storing infrastructure data long term is to summarize the data in hourly or daily chunks.

Observability tools are not limited to on-premise infrastructure monitoring. Tools such as Dynatrace, DataDog, NewRelic, and more have agents that collect infrastructure metrics from container and cloud platforms. Some vendors provide infrastructure monitoring tools specific to a particular infrastructure type, while others are wider in scope. For example, Splunk has an app called *Splunk App for Infrastructure* that provides a unified view of the entire infrastructure, including servers, applications, **Amazon Elastic Compute Cloud** (**Amazon EC2**), Kubernetes clusters, OpenShift clusters, Docker containers, and VMware vCenter Servers. It also has pre-built dashboards that provide visibility into key infrastructure metrics such as CPU usage, memory usage, network traffic, and more. You must choose a tool by assessing the extent to which you need the infrastructure data. Also, assess a tool based on ease of onboarding and offboarding devices on the tool based on your organization's overall tools and technology landscape. Agentless monitoring options are also available, which collect data via existing protocols such as **Simple Network Management Protocol (SNMP)**, **Windows Management Instrumentation (WMI)**, PowerShell, **Secure Shell Protocol (SSH)**, **representational state transfer** (**REST**) API, and NetFlow. A metric collection-based tool named Prometheus is widely used for containerized platforms where the microservice needs to expose data over an HTTP endpoint. It perfectly suits the nature of microservices. AIOps is slowly becoming the heart of infrastructure monitoring data collection, analysis, and tuning it to generate genuine alerts by adapting the thresholds per trends learned over time.

Depending on how the organization is set up, the observability team may or may not be responsible for facilitating the infrastructure data collection. At least for the legacy servers on-prem, most organizations have tools such as **System Center Operations Manager** (**SCOM**), OpManager, Nagios, MicroFocus, PRTG Network Monitor, Zabbix, and so on that already collect this data. The observability team can just tap into this data and stitch it up with application, business service, and customer experience data. Think rationally about infrastructure data collection from the cloud and containers; do not go for an all-in approach. Leverage what the vendor is providing. For example, CloudWatch and Azure Monitor expose infrastructure data and you can use their **user interface** (**UI**) to take a look at it. In the cloud, the provider is responsible for infrastructure, so you can limit your focus to ingesting metrics for the overall infrastructure health of your environment rather than the individual ephemeral components. The same applies to containers and pods as well.

Using infrastructure data

We have discussed the health and performance data that infrastructure generates and the methods to collect this data. Let us now take a look at how this data can be used at a broad level:

- **Understand the behavior of infrastructure and its impact on the application**

    Firstly, the observability team must set up a monitoring tool where data can be accessed, analyzed, and visualized. This helps in all phases of the **Software Development Life Cycle** (**SDLC**) as resource utilization can be monitored very closely, and adjustments can be made as needed.

- **Setup proactive alerting on resource utilization**

    Start with industry best practice as a threshold and then adjust it over time. These standard best practices recommend that we keep CPU utilization, memory utilization, and disk utilization below 80% and **input/output** (**I/O**) wait time at a minimum. Weigh your options in the monitoring tool to set up adaptive or dynamic thresholds rather than static ones. If the database team is notified of the fast filling of disk capacity well in time, they can act to avert some major issues.

- **Generate extensive reports on infrastructure health and performance status of the IT landscape using the collected data**

    To enable this, the same metrics must be collected from the same type of infrastructure or at least some common metrics should always be collected for a given type. Only then the observability team will be able to use this data consistently in their framework.

- **Create baselines for CPU, memory, and network utilization for every high-criticality host**

    This will give you quick insights and help you isolate infrastructure-related issues in case any incidents happen.

- **Predict and plan for infrastructure sizing and costs**

    Infrastructure utilization data can be correlated with system throughput and viewed over a timeline of the past three, six, or nine months to predict utilization and costs for upcoming months.

All applications need IT infrastructure to run on, and thus, it's critical to monitor the vitals of this layer. With modern architectures, the complexity of infrastructure is increasing and there are monitoring tools in the market to assist in covering the estate. Before buying, look at what your organization already has and whether it can be plugged into the observability tools. Even if you build your own custom infrastructure monitoring tool, consider that along with regular operations activities, it will also need additional effort to keep up with the changes in infrastructure features. One of the key outcomes of IT infrastructure monitoring is alerts that can help to nip the issues as they occur.

Having discussed infrastructure monitoring in detail, let's now take a look at the second layer of application monitoring – the application itself!

Data collection layer two – The application

The application, as we know, is a set of services that serve a business function. Monitoring an application is an important aspect in the realms of monitoring and observability. It typically involves monitoring the health of the overall application, the health of each individual service, the health of every component in a transaction flow, measuring **service level agreements (SLAs)** and **service level objectives (SLOs)**, and other fine-grained details. Observability focuses on overall health, the health of services, and measuring SLAs and SLOs. Fine-grained details monitoring is out of scope as observability focuses on establishing an overall picture of the business service and how it interacts with other services.

Data collection for monitoring the application

Applications are mostly custom designed and highly intrinsic to a particular business function within an organization. In our fictional company MK Tea, the code base for the packaging function will be different from any other tea organization. So, the velocity, volume, and variety of data that is collected greatly vary from application to application. The format of the data is not consistent either. However, data collection mechanisms remain the same – collect by installing an agent, collect over HTTPS, expose data as metrics and collect it using compatible agents, and collect via REST (volume bound). The most common method is via installing an agent. Layers at which application data is collected are application logs, **application performance monitoring (APM)**, and telemetry.

Collecting application log data

Data required for application monitoring is available in well-written log files. If an application uses a standard application such as a **WebSphere Application Server (WAS)** server, log files will be in standard format as published by the vendor. But in custom applications, these log formats are custom, and the monitoring and observability tools need to be trained to understand the data. Log data is in text format and contains information on why an event happened. It's a chronological representation of all activities that happen in an application. Some typical constructs of a log event are time and information on the activity. Log files were discussed in detail in *Chapter 2*.

APM data

APM data is collected by instrumenting the application to collect APM data via agents. Instrumentation involves enabling an application to generate metrics, logs, and traces as applicable. Libraries required for instrumentation of the applications vary across languages. APM tools easily collect APM data from applications with HTTP or HTTPS interfaces. Often, JavaScript is injected into the HTML code of the application for **Real User Monitoring** (**RUM**). Tool-specific agents are installed on the application servers to collect APM data. APM tools are purpose designed to collect and stitch together application processes by introducing `trace-id` or `span-id` if one is not available in the application. This `trace-id` is then used to map a customer journey or trace a transaction as it moves through various application services. APM tools can also clearly calculate the time spent by each transaction in a particular transaction. For example, it can identify how much time was spent in making the API call, page load, or fetching results from a database. With this granular information, developers and support teams are empowered to make informed decisions and drive the required changes in an application.

APM tools are available on-prem and in the cloud as **Software-as-a-Service** (**SaaS**) solutions. If APM data volumes and platform operations are a concern for your team, consider using SaaS solutions so that your teams can invest time in innovation, adoption of the tool, and integrations with external technologies.

Some benefits of APM data are as follows:

- Improved application performance as transactions can be tracked to each application component. If this data is available during the development and testing phase of an application, it will result in an optimized application and faster and higher-quality software releases.

- With visibility into resource usage, underlying data paths can be redesigned resulting in cost savings and increased revenue.

- The baseline of application behavior can be created automatically, which helps identify anomalies.

- The root cause of issues can be quickly identified with code-level monitoring and auto-fixed if possible, resulting in faster delivery. With the availability of process maps, the impact of an incident on other applications and customers can also be identified. Process maps (correlation between processes) are created by default by leveraging the auto-discovery of processes and services.

- Allows for more effective collaboration amongst teams, as the data speaks for itself through transaction tracing. Involved teams can share their findings more constructively.

- The data produced by legacy, distributed, cloud-native applications are different in nature, but APM tools can process all of this data and present the information in a standard format. Viewing all the data with the same lens allows time for focusing on the issue at hand rather than investing time in normalizing data across platforms.

- Automated alerts can be set up to enable effective reactive monitoring. Custom alerts can also be set up as required. Alerts provide timely information to the teams responsible for managing the application so that they can take required actions in time to maintain their SLAs.

Telemetry

In the IT world, telemetry was introduced roughly five years ago and is catching on fast with the advent of observability. It refers to collecting the data remotely and in the context of current applications and tools automatically. Telemetry data is a consistent measure of operational data that represents what is happening within an application. Having said that, telemetry data itself is not new, it has always existed. For example – voltage and temperature data from electrical sensors. Telemetry became popular in the IT world more recently. To collect telemetry data, you can either use application-specific collectors or libraries written in a particular language that can instrument application code to expose telemetry data over endpoints. You can also leverage collectors provided by the OpenTelemetry framework, which is a set of tools and libraries for collecting, processing, and exporting telemetry data from distributed applications. If you have microservices and hybrid architectures, choose your collection mechanism based on the vision and road map of your landscape. The instrumentation to collect telemetry data can be both automatic and manual. So, you can control the level of the data that gets collected.

The user experience can be improved with telemetry through application health checks, security monitoring, performance monitoring, and quality monitoring. When combined with AIOps (provided by most observability tools), this data can be used to detect anomalies and quickly establish baselines for normal behavior, sometimes in a matter of a few hours. AIOps is a definitive value on top of telemetry data and you don't have to worry about writing any code to enable this. It is a native feature of observability tools. The outcome of this integration is isolating the problem, faster incident resolution, and early detection of issues, all leading to an improved user experience.

In an ideal world, application monitoring would be plug-and-play where all application components generate telemetry data and observability tools can analyze and correlate it across applications and platforms. It would provide data for observability from the time the application starts up. Observability tools would also have standard dashboards that light up when data starts coming in. Thus, observability implementation becomes automatic and achievable with minimal effort. Until we reach the utopia, we need to work on collecting data from each application bit by bit. Focus on collecting information-rich logs that can help identify the root cause of the problem and designing interfaces and systems for capturing metrics and traces. Keep in mind that storage is finite and expensive. So, collecting everything from everywhere and storing it for longer durations is not a feasible option. Interactive dashboards can be built using the application monitoring data sets that provide deep insights to the developers, testing teams, support teams, and executives.

To summarize, application logs, APM data, and telemetry will provide more than 97% monitoring coverage for all types of applications. Other datasets can come from network monitoring or any external components. If your application uses a third-party vendor or an external SaaS solution, you might want to either plug in their dataset or analyze a feed from their monitoring system into your observability toolsets.

We hope that you now understand the two most common layers of application monitoring – infrastructure and application. Let's move on to the third layer.

Data collection layer three – the business service

Observability has evolved from infrastructure and application monitoring, discussed in the previous section. However, neither infrastructure nor application monitoring has the business context of IT systems that they monitor. Due to this lack of visibility, business and product managers cannot identify the business impact due to IT system outages, the user experience of the services, and other metrics that represent the health of the services that the IT system offers.

In a modern distributed architecture, infrastructure and application layers are becoming much more opaque as organizations increasingly adopt distributed architecture, cloud platforms and containers. This architecture provides organizations with increased agility and efficiency, faster deployments, more automation opportunities, and increased collaboration. While the organizations adopt these practices, they can pretty much outsource the infrastructure and, in some cases, applications as well in the form of SaaS. This poses a unique challenge to organizations on how to monitor and guarantee the health of business services. Business service observability overcomes this challenge by monitoring a business service from end to end and enables the business teams to monitor the business **key performance indicators (KPIs)** such as sales volume, business conversion rates, search versus buy, user experience score, and so on. As long as the business service health can be maintained within acceptable limits, where and how the infrastructure and application stacks are managed becomes irrelevant. This enables the service providers to outsource the infrastructure to specialist infrastructure providers such as AWS, GCP, or Azure; and in some cases it enables them to also outsource infrastructure and applications to vendors. This allows the service providers to concentrate solely on building and managing the business services.

The main sources of performance data for business services are logs, traces, and metrics from the application stack itself. Along with the application performance metrics, applications can generate data related to the business services it serves. In a highly observable application architecture, end-to-end tracing of services can be achieved by adopting a vendor-neutral open standard for distributed tracing such as open tracing that helps developers to instrument, collect, and visualize trace data from complex distributed systems. Similarly, adopting industry-standard logging formats can standardize the logs and provide consistency in data generation across the stack. In the case of legacy applications or scenarios where the application architecture cannot be changed; tracing and business service monitoring can be provided by APM via implementing the required instrumentation. However, the goal should be to incorporate the industry standards for logging and tracing into application architecture for a high level of maturity and consistency across the technology stack.

This section will guide you in developing an understanding of the business service and various customer experience monitoring approaches such as **digital experience monitoring (DEM)**, **synthetic transaction monitoring (STM)**, **endpoint monitoring**, and **real user monitoring (RUM)**.

Digital experience monitoring

DEM is a method of collecting and processing metrics that are related to the customer journey performed by an end customer. These metrics can be used to determine the quality of digital interactions, measure customer experience, and real user experience to validate the availability of digital functions and service availability across various digital interfaces such as the web, tablets, mobiles, and so on. While the infrastructure and application monitoring observe a service from a service provider's point of view, DEM enhances observability by providing an end-user perceptive.

The rest of this section outlines common practices used in DEM, which help you in recording your customer's digital experience when they use the IT services that you provide.

Synthetic transaction monitoring

STM tools are used to simulate actual user interaction in a digital service by traversing through a customer journey from end to end. Various parameters such as response time, latency, packet loss, availability, and so on are calculated and compared against the established baseline. This type of monitoring can be used to replicate various real-world customer scenarios such as multiple geographical locations, different types of networks, browsers, multiple devices, and so on. STM can also be extended to monitor API interfaces that are used by downstream applications/services to fulfill their respective functions.

Endpoint monitoring

Endpoint monitoring is a method to monitor the last-mile device of a service. The last-mile device can be a physical device such as a laptop, tablet, or mobile, or a virtual device such as a virtual desktop or a cloud computer. For almost all the digital services that a customer consumes, the customer uses one of these endpoints, and poor performance of these devices can result in a poor experience. By collecting metrics from these last-mile endpoint devices, the service provider can quickly distinguish the issues between the service provider side and the customer endpoint side.

Real user monitoring

RUM is a monitoring process that captures performance metrics related to real user interaction with an application. It's commonly used to measure the user experience, identify and resolve frontend performance issues, analyze service usage, collect custom metrics related to the customer journey, and so on. The output of RUM can be used by the UI developer to improve the design and streamline the service interface. The most common method of real user monitoring is to ingest codes to the user interfaces, which will collect the relevant metrics and stream them back to the service provider for processing. For example, JavaScript code can be embedded in web pages to collect RUM data from browser-based applications while libraries can be used to collect and stream RUM data from mobile applications or set-top boxes.

Now let us take the example of the e-commerce website and see how each of these techniques can help. Let's consider the service called "Buying a Product". The whole customer journey includes several high-level functions such as the following:

- Providing the customer with a list of products to choose from

- Once the product is selected, providing a payment option

- Packaging and shipping to the customer's location

Each of these functions in the customer journey is fulfilled by an application service, and some of them are outsourced to a third party, such as delivery. For a highly observable service, the order needs to be tracked and monitored end to end to make sure the order is fulfilled within the agreed SLA.

The application stack underpinning the website can introduce open tracing standards so that when the customer selects the product, an ID (`trace-id`) is created, and this ID is passed on to every subsequent function managed by the relevant application stack, such as payments, packaging, and delivery. In each of these functions, a new ID is created (`span-id`), which will be used to track the specific operation such as one `span-id` for payments, one for packaging, and then one for delivery. So, with one `trace-id`, the entire process from end to end can be tracked and each function can be tracked using its relevant `span-id`. This is explained in the following diagram:

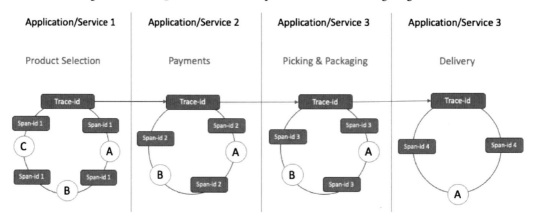

Figure 4.2 – Correlating functions using a common Trace-id

By adopting a logging standard or by using industry standards such as OpenTelemetry, applications can be programmed to generate performance data related to each of these functions and report it along with the trace and span ID of the customer journey. When `trace-id` and performance data are combined, then for each customer order, the performance of each function of the order can be measured individually. This performance measure can then be aggregated to provide end-to-end performance metrics of an individual order. The same method can be applied to other services such as returning faulty products, order cancellation, and so on.

Now we can measure the performance of the service from the service provider side, let's see how the user side can be monitored. Since all the DEM methods that are described previously overlap in capabilities, for this use case, RUM would be the ideal choice. The e-commerce website and mobile app can both be built to include code and libraries to collect RUM data and stream it back to the service provider. This data will provide insights related to page load time, latency click streams, user navigation paths, and the performance difference between devices, which can be used to monitor the digital interface of the service and help in designing better web and app interfaces. The e-commerce website is used by customers globally and needs to measure global performance, implementing synthetic monitoring might be useful. Synthetic probes can be hosted in multiple locations across the globe and initiate a transaction and measure the performance for comparative analysis. Endpoint monitoring may not be an apt solution in this case as the customers might be using many types of devices, and installing endpoint monitoring agents in all of these devices is not feasible.

A good example of an endpoint monitoring use case is a video streaming service that uses a set-top box on the customer premise. In this case, an endpoint monitoring agent can be installed by default in the set-top box to collect the performance metrics such as page load time, buffering rate, packet drops, network speed, and so on, and stream back to the service provider for tracking and analysis.

It can take your organization some time to focus on business service and customer experience monitoring. You can start with the applications that are end-customer facing and then apply the learnings to other applications. You might also need to invest in upskilling your team to enable them to get started with this third layer of monitoring. The fourth layer (the last one in the context of this book) is organization, which overarches the other three layers. It will be discussed in the next section.

Data collection layer four – The organization

In almost all organizations, monitoring is done in a very ad-hoc manner. A centralized monitoring team sources a few monitoring tools based on requirements and provides the service to the rest of the organization. Application and business teams, as and when required, will reach out to the monitoring team to implement monitoring and alerting using these tools. Certain technology teams will even buy their own specific monitoring products for their technology stacks. For example, SCOM is used for Windows fleets, HP-**Operations Bridge Manager (OBM)** for Unix fleets, and so on. This can result in a tools-galore situation in the organization. As we have mentioned before, for implementing observability and especially for a high level of maturity, this ad-hoc approach will not deliver the desired results. It requires observability to be implemented at all levels (infrastructure, application, and business layers) in a consistent manner and across all the applications to attain service-level visibility. To achieve this, first organizations should have a good understanding of the IT assets they own, their relationships, and a governance process to make sure that this information is systematically tracked and updated regularly.

All organizations maintain an inventory of software and hardware assets they own and operate. This inventory is generally called a **configuration management database (CMDB)**, which has been discussed in detail in *Chapter 2*.

Using CMDB, questions such as which monitoring tools are deployed to which CIs, and hence to which application, how many CIs are not monitored, and what are the dependent CIs or applications for a business service can be answered. By combining CMDB data with an observability governance process, organizations can standardize the observability tools, avoid duplicate data collections, and also systematically deploy the monitoring and observability tools across the organization, thus maintaining the reliability of the observability outcomes.

Other important information sources that the organization needs to record and maintain are process maps, user experience maps, customer journey maps, service aggregate maps, and so on. These have also been discussed in detail in *Chapter 2*. These maps will show the dependencies between various components and are also used as a template for building visualization, where the observability data can be overlayed to provide the end-to-end health view.

Let's go back to the example of the e-commerce website and the "Buying a Product" service. CMDB will provide a list of CIs per application (product selection, payments, and packaging and delivery). Using the list we can track the monitoring coverage and tools used. The coverage information ensures reliability and provides confidence in the observability data and the related outcomes. CMDB also provides information regarding dependent applications or CI for the service, which can be used to identify various components in the end-to-end service view. With the service view and the observability data from all the layers, a completely observable system can be built.

Generally, the outcome of an observability monitoring solution will be a set of visualizations (dashboards) and/or events or alerts to an alerting system when an anomaly or an issue is detected. All these outcomes will be discussed in detail in *Chapter 5*. In a highly mature observability architecture, if the data (logs, traces, and metrics) and data collection methods are standardized, CMDB dependency mapping can be used to automatically calculate the end-to-end performance of the service. When a new service is implemented in the organization, as soon as the standardized observability data and CMDB mapping data are made available, an end-to-end service monitoring solution can be programmatically created, thereby fully automating the process. CMDB mapping data or maps from the process bank can act as a template for the visualization, and SLOs, SLAs, and SLIs can be used as thresholds for alerting and eventing.

Summary

You may have heard the saying, "data is the new oil." Even though this tagline was framed for another context, it's true for observability, as it is the oil that drives the observability engine.

The data collection layers that we have addressed in this chapter provide a simple way to divide the observability landscape. Each of these layers needs to be individually analyzed and reviewed carefully in the context of your organization and catalog the data required to achieve the observability goals, one application at a time. We recommend doing that in the order outlined in this chapter – infrastructure, application, business service, and lastly, organization. The complexity of data collection increases with each layer. Simple application architecture requires a simple setup, and as application complexity increases, multiple tools and methods need to be employed to get full stack observability. This understanding emphasizes the standardization of observability tools and processes across the applications and prepares the observability teams to handle a diverse dataset..

5
Observability Outcomes: Dashboards, Alerts, and Incidents

Till now, we have focused on building the foundation for observability. First, we talked about observability and challenges with traditional monitoring techniques. We also introduced you to the data required for setting up observability, such as logs, metrics, and traces, along with the **configuration management database** (**CMDB**). Using the data, we then discussed KPIs, service views, and layers of the IT landscape at which observability can be implemented and how it can be done. Along with all this, we also made you aware of the common challenges faced while implementing observability in an organization.

In this chapter, we will use all these foundations to discuss how we can build something that helps you and your customers in reaping the benefits of the efforts that you have put into building the observability setup. You will come across the following terms in this chapter:

- **Dashboards**: This is the visual representation of the analysis done on available data
- **Alerts**: These are proactive notifications that alert about something that needs the attention of the team responsible for managing the asset
- **Incidents**: An unplanned interruption governed by **Information Technology Infrastructure Library** (**ITIL**) processes (this is introduced later in the chapter)

We will discuss each of these terms in detail in the context of observability. What do they mean, what are the benefits, who sets them up, and who is the consumer?

So, let's get cracking!

Getting to know dashboards

Dashboards represent collective insights on what is happening in the IT environment, the application's performance, forecasts on usage and capacity, business metrics, customer experience, and many more. If developed with focus, they can easily help analyze, track, visualize, and display the underlying data. A typical dashboard will have as many panels as can fit on a standard screen. Each panel represents a fragment of information.

Let's say, if a dashboard was built for MK Tea to monitor the shipping of packed tea, it would have the following panels:

- Packets ready versus required by type
- The health of quality **key performance indicators (KPIs)**
- Number of orders fulfilled
- Number of orders pending
- Number of orders in transit
- Order details

Dashboards can be static based on a predefined set of requirements or interactive which allows users to provide inputs and also analyze and explore the data to find answers to questions that were previously unknown. As in the previous example, the first five panels are static, and the last panel is interactive as it takes input from the user and then shows results. There is another feature called **drill down** in dashboards. As the name suggests, it allows users to click on a panel and get further information on that metric. Continuing the example of the MK Tea Shipping Stats dashboard, when a user clicks on the fifth panel, *No of orders in transit*, they are shown information on the number of orders reaching in a day, in seven days, and the number of orders that are running delayed. Drill downs can be configured to present information on the same dashboard or on a completely new one.

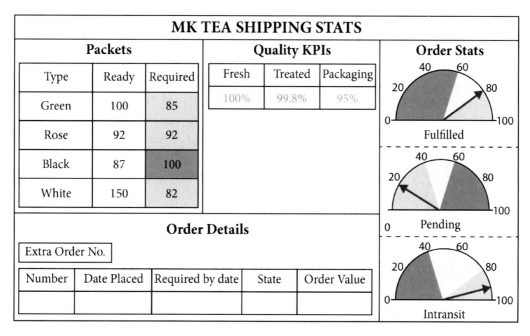

Figure 5.1 – The MK Tea Shipping Stats dashboard

The following dashboard presents a drill down of the *Orders in Transit* panel shown in the preceding figure:

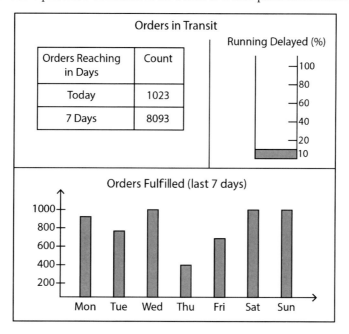

Figure 5.2 – The MK Tea Orders in Transit details dashboard

Considering the preceding example, it is self-explanatory that dashboards help observe an application or a business service. It can be as simple as the one that trends on CPU utilization and as complex as tracing a customer journey in a distributed application that has a transaction rate of 200 unique customers per second. The amount of value that is delivered by the dashboard totally depends on the quality of the data available. Good analytical skills of the developer also contributes to building a meaningful dashboard. Data is the logs, metrics, and traces we discussed in *Chapter 2*. Requirements are given by the customers in general. However, some customers are not clear on what they need initially and they start with one or two panels. As their experience with the dashboard evolves, they will have more requirements to deliver insights for their application. This happens regularly with a lot of customers. Therefore, a developer should not only be skilled in configuring the tool or writing code to build a dashboard, but they should also be adept at understanding the customer's background and building panels for them. For example, business executives will not be interested in the health of the database servers; they would rather like to know whether traffic on the website is increasing after the recent facelift. In most environments, customers can create their own dashboards through prior experience and self learning or with minimal help from the observability team.

Dashboards are built on observability tools. Some tools need to be configured by the developers or users to build a dashboard, while some tools come with pre-built dashboards that light up when data is made available. Most modern tools have a combination of both. They have pre-built dashboards to present general insights such as the health of the server and application, open connections, resource utilization, and so on. They also allow the developers to get as creative as possible using the tool-specific query language, configuration parameters, common languages, or data formats such as JSON, XML, HTML, and so on.

The relevant application teams are ultimately responsible for creating and maintaining a dashboard, with the help and support of the observability team. In case the relevant application team does not have the right skills, the observability team can step in to create the dashboards until the application teams can acquire the necessary skills and are ready to be self-sufficient. With time, a lot of dashboards become obsolete. For example, if an application that was hosted on-prem moves to the cloud, then the dashboard configured for on-prem will no longer be relevant. This is just an example; there are thousands of such scenarios in the real world. It is the responsibility of the application team to make the relevant changes to observability dashboards to keep them up to date. If possible, observability teams should try periodically to scan the setup for unused dashboards, reach out to the relevant application **subject matter expert** (**SME**) and take action to either decommission the dashboard or enhance it to suit the observability needs of the application. Also, these scanning results can be great inputs for observability maturity reports as observability adoption metrics, which we will discuss in *Chapter 7*. In summary, the life cycle of dashboards can be represented as follows:

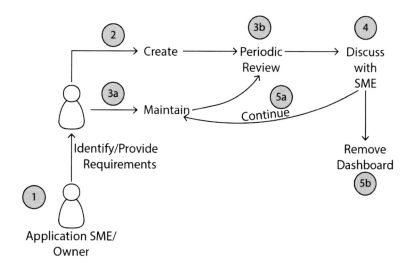

Figure 5.3 – The life cycle of a dashboard

You may argue that dashboards are also used in monitoring. So, what is special about what we are doing in observability? The answer is, there is no difference at all in the relevance of dashboards, how they are built, who builds them, and who is responsible for maintaining them. Since observability is also called supercharged monitoring, observability and monitoring share some areas such as data collection, dashboards, alerts, and incidents. If you are working towards uplifting monitoring practice to observability, you can retain and reuse all your dashboards. In the next sections, we will discuss alerts and incidents; both are in the same category as dashboards when discussing setting up observability. You can retain most of the alerts and incidents that you might have in the monitoring setup.

Introducing alerts and incidents

Dashboards are visual tools to enhance understanding of the IT landscape and everything within. While dashboards present a lot of information in processed and crunched format, are easy to consume, and can be built for both technical and business audiences at different levels, they require a set of human eyes to watch them, read the information, and infer meaning from it. There is no limit to the number of dashboards that can be built, but there is a limit to the number of human eyes that can be employed to look at them and the number of screens on which they can be displayed. Does it mean that it is impossible to use the dashboards? Not at all! As explained in the previous section, dashboards should be built specifically for a purpose and audience and should be maintained as long as they stay relevant.

In an IT landscape, although you have the dashboards to provide you leads on what is happening in it, it is more of a "come-to-me" approach. You need to watch a dashboard to get information. There are scenarios where the team responsible needs to be notified immediately so that it can take corrective action. Let's look at an example to understand this. MK Tea has a dashboard that measures the `RollingMachine.TeaRolledVolume` metric for all the tea-rolling machines and trends it against the maximum possible performance for the particular model. (This metric was discussed in *Chapter 2*, in the *Metrics* section). On a working day, the throughput of one of the tea-rolling machines starts to drop during lunchtime. The staff responsible for reading the dashboard are away and the problem remains unattended for an hour. By the time staff are back, throughput has dropped by 50%. This causes slowness in the entire production line and delays in packaging, shipping, and delivery. It's a clear dollar loss for the company.

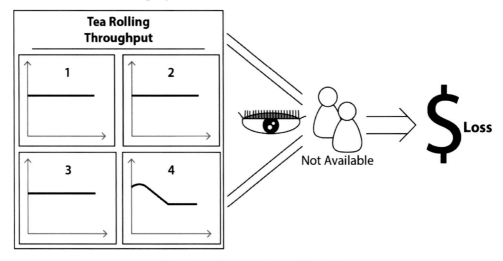

Figure 5.4 – Limitation of dashboards

Here, the dashboard provided the information, but the value of that information was lost because it was not consumed effectively. This is where alerts and incidents come into the picture. They automatically notify the responsible staff when a problem is detected in the system. Continuing the previous example, if the technician had been notified when the throughput of the machine dropped by 10%, the situation could have been handled better. They could have fixed the problem quickly, saving time and money.

In observability implementations, when you open up your services and infrastructure for monitoring, dashboards alone will not help. Instead, you will need to carefully set up alerts on the important features of the services, applications, and infrastructure so that timely actions can be taken to resolve the problems that may arise. Here, you can leverage KPIs that were discussed in *Chapter 2*, in the *Identifying KPIs* section. We also shared information on Google golden signals in the same section.

A common question is about the difference between alerts and incidents. In many organizations, these terms are used interchangeably. A quick Google search defines an incident in accordance with its literal term: when something catastrophic happens in the IT environment and impacts a large percentage of staff or customers. However, this literal definition is never used in day-to-day operations in the IT landscape. Instead, throughout this book, we will stick to the modern implementation of alerts and incidents. Industry-wide, it is believed that alerts and incidents are a result of the cause that occurs in the IT environment. Most modern tools maintain a difference between alerts and incidents, but they all agree that the cause will be called an event.

An event can either be detected by the application or service where it originates and self-reports directly to the **IT Service Management (ITSM)** tool or to an observability tool which uses this event to detect the issue in the application or service, generate another event suitable for the ITSM tool, and passes it to the ITSM tool. The ITSM tools will receive these events and record them either as alerts or incidents. An alert can be informative or just a proactive message for reference. It becomes an incident when it indicates an unplanned interruption in the IT environment. Based on the operational requirement, alert and incident notifications can be sent out to the responsible teams and are always tracked under a defined **service level agreement (SLA)**. The only difference is in the nature of the information that is conveyed through these notifications. Incidents always indicate that something is not working as expected, whereas, in the case of an alert, it can just be an update or a notification to draw the user's attention to important information. In ITIL, there are volumes of information on how the SLA of an incident should be managed. This book is not focused on that. For the uninitiated, ITIL is a series of practices in ITSM that are used worldwide as standards. The key message that we want to convey is that observability tools generate the events and pass them on. The support team consumes these events either as alerts or incidents based on the characteristics of the event. What happens within an event management tool (ITSM), how it is set up, and so on, needs to be left to the ITSM engineers. Observability and support engineers should concentrate on understanding the difference in message that alerts and incidents convey and creating an operational mechanism to respond appropriately to situations that alerts and incidents indicate.

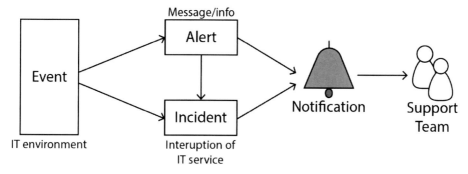

Figure 5.5 – Understanding events, alerts, and incidents

Let's understand events, alerts, and incidents in the context of MK Tea. In a tea processing and packaging plant, the last stage of the packaging machine generates an event every hour updating the number of packets that have been packed. The observability tool consumes this information and can generate an alert if the number of packets deviates from the expected numbers. This is just information to flag that there was a deviation.

In the same example, if the number of packets has significantly dropped or completely stopped, it indicates that an outage in production has happened. This will be captured by the observability tool, and it will generate an incident, sending a notification to the technician because a disruption of services has happened. It cannot be a friendly message.

Now that you have a fair understanding of events, alerts, and incidents, let's take a look at how alerts and incidents are created. Let's look at the most basic method using logs:

1. The application that experiences an issue in its functioning writes a log entry describing the problem.

2. This log is consumed by a log management tool. This tool scrapes the logs at fixed intervals on a schedule to look for the records in logs that indicate some issue.

3. The tool creates an event that is further consumed by the tool that can generate alerts and trigger incidents.

The same can be implemented using metrics or traces. Observability tools such as **Application and Performance Monitoring** (**APM**) tools do not depend on the applications to provide the data to identify an event. These tools can detect an event that happened in the IT environment where it is deployed and can raise an alert or incident based on the configured rules.

Here is a high-level visual representation of everything that has been discussed in this section:

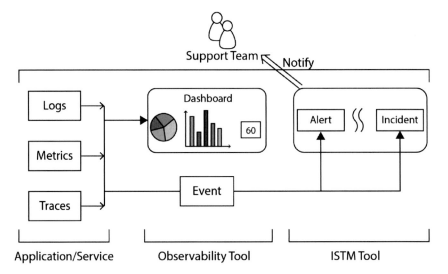

Figure 5.6 – Data, dashboards, and alerting

> **Note**
>
> The common concepts that we discussed here related to events, alerts, and incidents apply to all modern observability tools that are capable of generating alerts and incidents. We recommend familiarizing yourself with ITIL processes if you do not know them already.

Alerts and incidents play a major role in observability implementations as they help the application SMEs maintain the health of the application. In the next section, we will look at alerts and incidents in more detail.

Alerts and incidents – the finer details

We introduced alerts and incidents in the previous section. They are like wake-up calls about anything that deserves attention in an IT environment when something needs to be notified or something is not behaving as expected. In this section, we will answer the following fundamental questions:

- At what point should an alert be set up?

- What should be the frequency of the alert?

- How should the alert behave for the first and consecutive events?

- Who are the consumers of alerts?

That is a lot to understand, and as simple as it may sound, it needs a team of people with varied skills to identify alert touchpoints, develop them, respond to them, and keep them relevant. An observability team needs members with all these skills, and for those members to work closely with application SMEs to create quality alerts.

Let's start answering the questions one by one.

At what point should an alert be set up?

Any event in the IT environment that needs the attention of the team responsible for managing an asset's health is a candidate for setting up an alert. Some examples of such events are the occurrence of error codes in logs, drop in throughput, increase in CPU or disk utilization, absence of hits on the website, increase in transaction times, data not being received, and many more. Alert touchpoints don't always have to be technical; they can also be business related. For example, a drop in expected sale numbers during Black Friday, a downward trend of fewer unique customers visiting the website, overall service status, and many more. You can also leverage the KPIs for setting up alerts. It is always a good idea to set up alerts when the health of a KPI changes. While the application SMEs will always push for setting up alerts for every error code and possible unfriendly scenario in their application, the observability team members need to conduct a conversation with the application SME on the relevance of the alerts being set up. Common questions to consider when setting up an alert are as follows:

- What does this error code indicate?

- What is the impact on the application if the error is not addressed?

- Do you need to just be notified of the occurrence, or do you need to track it under an SLA via incidents?

Such questions push the SME to re-think whether they really need that alert.

An observability tool should be capable of supporting thousands of alerts. As observability matures, the observability team will need to periodically assess the capacity of the tools and keep them relevant to the technical and business needs. The observability team is responsible for guiding the application SME, help them in setting up the alert in the tool, and periodically checking whether the alert is useful.

What should be the frequency of the alert?

As you know by now, alerts are the results of the events that happen in the IT environment. Observability tools constantly look for these causes and generate alerts. Frequency determines how often the tool should look for these causes. For example, a server that is configured with a small disk tends to get full for multiple reasons. As the disk space approaches 80%, the performance of certain business functions starts dipping. The workaround to resolve the problem is simple and can take only three to eight minutes. Waiting for the disk usage to reach 80% will allow very little room for the SME to resolve the problem. In this case, set up an alert that runs every 10 minutes and checks for disk usage reaching 60%, which is 20% below the point where problems start to occur. Here, 60% becomes the threshold for the alert; it's the usage value at which the alert should be raised. To identify the threshold, the observability team needs to sit with the application SMEs and discuss two main points:

1.   What is the tolerance of the system? To what point can the application keep running without any issues for a given scenario?

2.   How much time does it take to resolve the problem in the best- and worst-case scenarios?

From our decade-long experience in the monitoring space, we've found that a lot of application SMEs want alerts to be run every minute so that they get notified of the issue as soon as it happens. It sounds fancy but is mostly useless. One-minute alerts consume a lot of resources on the observability tool without driving any meaningful results. Asking the two preceding questions will help you to identify how to configure the alert. Question 1 will help you to identify the correct threshold, and question 2 will help you calculate the correct frequency. If an issue takes a minimum of 15 minutes to resolve, there is no point in generating an alert and notifying SMEs of the problem every 2 minutes. Instead, notify on the first occurrence and then notify again after 15 minutes if the event occurs again.

How to manage alerts?

Once the alerts and incidents are set up, the question arises – how to effectively manage them. One of the common issues with observability or enhanced monitoring we have noticed is alerts and/or incidents galore to be consumed by the operations teams. This mainly results from the traditional ways of working, where operation teams only want to be notified when there is a problem or an outage. As mentioned in an earlier chapter, the focus of observability is to detect and resolve the issue before it becomes an outage. Hence in a mature observability environment, we should be seeing a surge in the number of alerts (proactive indication of a problem) resulting in a reduced number of incidents, as problems are identified using alerts and resolved before it becomes an outage or incident. Hence managing this surge in notifications becomes very important to the success of the observability implementation. There is no single solution to this problem. We have to employ multiple strategies to manage this. Some of them are described in the following list:

- **ITSM event correlation**: All modern-day ITSM tools have an event correlation feature. In the ITSM context, an *event* is any notification that the ITSM tools receive from the IT environment, and in the observability context and also in the context of this book, these events are alerts and incidents. Please keep this differentiation in mind while reading this section. ITSM event (alerts and incidents) correlation is about understanding the relationship between various event (alerts and incidents) that originates from the IT system and identifying and/or prioritizing the events (alerts and incidents) that can cause more damage to the IT services. For example, in MK Tea, an alert indicating an increase in the temperature of the packaging machine can be a one-off event. However, the same alert correlated with a drop in the number of tea packages produced indicates a potential service disruption scale issue that needs to be addressed on priority. We strongly recommend consulting with ITSM experts within your organization to implement ITSM event correlation techniques to reduce the noise that observability can potentially cause.

- **Alert/incident suppression and throttling**: The intention behind notification is to capture the attention of the relevant engineers and support personnel regarding an issue. The key to the success of the notification is the clarity of the message, the appropriate level of priority, and a proper escalation path; not the number of notifications that you receive. All the modern observability tools provide suppression or throttling facilities to reduce the repeated firing of the same alerts or incidents to prevent the overloading of the ISTM tools and notification systems. Different types of suppression type of methods can be employed to attain the optimum notification, such as time-based, type-based, source-based, and so on, where each of these attributes (time, type, and source) is used to create rules to prevent repeated firing of the same information or to provide a pause before notifications are fired again. These features can also be implemented in the ITSM tools, as most of the ITSM tools also provide these features. In addition, auto-linking the alerts or incidents with a change management record for a particular IT system can also help to suppress the alerts originating from an application undergoing a planned change activity.

- **Regular review and optimization**: The other method the application team should employ is to constantly review and, if required, optimize the alerts and incidents configured. As the operations teams manage applications for a longer period, they should be able to develop a series of operational parameters within which the application or service should operate to maintain stability and operational integrity. The operations teams should use the knowledge gained from this experience to periodically review and tune the alert and incident thresholds, configurations, and baselines, cover newly discovered blind spots, adjust the priority levels, and so on. If you are employing machine learning for predictive alerts, make sure to train the machine learning model periodically to improve the accuracy of the prediction. These constant reviews and optimization will help in reducing the noise.

So, who are the consumers of alerts?

Application teams are responsible for setting up the alerts working in conjunction with the observability engineers if required, and they are the primary consumers of these alerts. As alerts provide information on the health of the application or its related services, when things go south, it is the responsibility of the application team to look into the issue and resolve it. Here, the responsibilities of the observability team include: helping application team in setting up the alert, maintaining the health of the observability platform so that alerts keep running as expected, and ensuring the application SMEs are notified in time. Application teams may get multiple incidents in a day about different kinds of issues in the application. All incidents are associated with a severity level that defines the time in which the incident must be resolved. The highest-priority incidents are resolved first. A good quality CMDB (discussed in *Chapter 2*) helps in assessing the impact of an incident on other applications and services. In case of high-severity incidents, the keepers of the associated applications are also notified so they can monitor their application and help identify the full scope of the ongoing incident.

In observability implementations, the team must periodically assess whether the existing alerts and incidents are helpful. For example, are support teams ignoring them or finding them useful? This can be done by discussing with the users or by keeping a tab on the user's comments on the alerts and incidents. If you often see incidents being closed with comments such as "false alarm, to be ignored", then this is a red flag and should be addressed as quickly as possible. Discuss with the users and then either disable the alert or tweak it so that it becomes helpful.

Time and again in this chapter, we have mentioned that observability tools can help set up dashboards, alerts, and incidents. Some common tools you can explore for this purpose have been discussed in *Chapter 9*.

Observability consumers – self healing

Self-healing infrastructure or applications or services is considered to be the next step in **artificial intelligence for IT operations** (**AIOps**) and automation. By implementing observability, developers and engineers can generate and ingest a large amount of data related to an application or a service. Using this data, the observability tools can detect a deviation in performance and instability in service and also identify potential outages. Once these are detected, this information can be passed on to a downstream system such as an automation tool to invoke workflows that can be used to resolve or recover the health of the application or services.

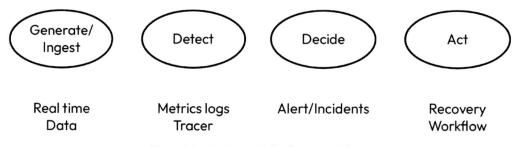

Figure 5.7 – An observability future workflow

Shell (**sh**) and Python scripts are commonly used to speed up recovery during outages by automating recovery steps such as restarting servers, diverting traffic to a different set of endpoints, clearing the cache, and so on. All these steps can be fully automated by invoking dedicated workflows for a detected scenario. Self-healing/recovery IT systems are still at a very nascent stage of development but have immense potential, and observability outcomes can be an enabler for this feature.

Summary

Dashboards, alerts, and incidents are the objects that provide visual insights and notifications for the IT landscape. Observability tools can be configured to keep your team up to date with even the slightest variations on infrastructure, application, or business layers, and overall performance.

In this chapter, you learned how to use dashboards to keep watch on what is going on in your IT environment, monitor the data by comparing against KPIs or error conditions and generate events, and plug these events into an alert and incident management tool. While sending all events and setting up notifications on every alert is always tempting, be conscious of the usability of too many alerts. Focus on adopting techniques such as correlation and suppression to control the number of notifications that are sent out to the teams responsible for resolving the issues. For a more high-level understanding of some of the concepts that were briefly covered in this chapter, you can read up on ITIL and ITSM.

Part 2 – Planning and Implementation

This part provides guidance on implementing observability in an organization. It offers advice on analyzing an organization's culture and developing a governance model to support observability. It also introduces Maturity Levels and provides guardrails to guide the reader through the implementation process, emphasizing the importance of required skills. This part also identifies stakeholders and provides a **Responsible, Support, Consulted and Informed (RASCI)** matrix to clarify their responsibilities and ownership. Finally, this part guides readers on selecting appropriate observability tools and offers guidance on what to consider before buying, building, or leveraging observability tools. Overall, readers will get a comprehensive roadmap for implementing observability in an organization.

This part has the following chapters:

- *Chapter 6, Gauging the Organization for Observability Implementation*
- *Chapter 7, Achieving and Measuring Observability Success*
- *Chapter 8, Identifying the Stakeholders*
- *Chapter 9, Deciding the Tools for Observability*

6

Gauging the Organization for Observability Implementation

Does my organization need observability? If yes, what approach should I take to meet the business goals? These are the questions you should ask before starting this journey, as the size, organization culture, services offered, and so on will determine the effort, technology choices, and investment required for the observability journey.

In all the chapters so far, we have discussed technological aspects of observability. We started with the *What was before observability* section, then we discussed, logs, metrics, traces, and the different layers of the application at which data is collected, and in the previous chapter, we talked about dashboards, alerts, and incidents. This chapter steps away from technology and looks at the organization itself. You may have great ideas, funding, and people for implementing observability, but if your organization itself is not conducive to changes, nothing will work as expected. So, we decided to center your thoughts on the organization itself and address some of the key organizational traits and practices the organization leaders should consider and nurture for the observability implementation to succeed.

Before we get into analyzing the nature and behavior of an organization, let's recall the key benefits of observability from *Chapter 1* so that we can clearly discuss the challenges a particular type of organization may face as it progresses through its observability journey:

- Correlated applications that deliver higher business value

- Improved customer experience driving customer loyalty

- Tools rationalization for improved ROI

- Focuses on not just tech but also the process

- Data noise is converted into actionable insights

- Foundation for a self-healing architecture

You can refer to the detailed explanation of each of these benefits in *Chapter 1*.

Organization and culture

An organization's culture can be considered as its personality, more or less the same as humans and animals. Similar to personality, culture comprises of values and beliefs that define the organization and influence how an organization operates, and how employees and management behave, interact, and respond to situations. Thus, this is what makes an organization unique. All the most successful companies have their own unique culture, and most of these successful cultures focus on the organization and its goals, not on individuals. These organizations reinforce the values and beliefs regularly and establish practices and policies to encourage adoption, communicate these values regularly, and reward behaviors that are in line with the culture.

There are many types of organizational culture in the corporate world. Many of these cultures are carefully crafted based on the needs of the organization, some of them evolved over time, and some of them are heavily influenced by the industry they belong to. Anthropologists, who are experts in culture and human behavior, generally categorize corporate culture into four categories, as discussed in this resource: `https://www.ocai-online.com/about-the-Organizational-Culture-Assessment-Instrument-OCAI`. These categories are as follows:

- **Clan culture (collaborate culture)**: A family-oriented organization, where leaders are considered mentors, and co-workers are considered family members. The focus is on teamwork, loyalty, and frameworks, and generally works on consensus. These organizations are fast in achieving benefits that thrive on collaboration but make slow progress in the areas where a strong uni-directional approach is needed for driving business. Open source projects or community projects are great examples of this, as people stick together based on ideas, ideology, or inspired by a leader, and collaborate with a sense of purpose to achieve an outcome.

- **Control culture (hierarchy culture)**: As the name suggests, a very hierarchical organization, with a well-developed organizational structure and processes. The focus is on providing a stable, reliable organization that can deliver results. The scope of change is quite restricted. Implementing any disruptive change such as observability is very challenging in such organizations, as it requires a mindset shift, breaking down silos to make operations transparent, and quickly adopting new technology. Financial institutions or government organizations are generally an example of the control culture, where their operations are heavily influenced by the regulatory and compliance processes.

- **Create culture (adhocracy culture)**: Mostly popular with start-ups, where employees are encouraged to create and innovate without any restrictions on processes or traditions. The focus is on agility, risk-taking, experimentation, and learning from mistakes, and thus aims to achieve long-term growth by creating new products and services. Observability requires patience as it evolves over time; it's not a *build-and-forget* kind of implementation. Start-ups will definitely make headway with their focus on technology and automation. Examples of create culture organizations are start-ups in any industry; recent examples are Tesla, Afterpay, and so on, where organizations push boundaries and must continuously learn, adapt, and evolve to achieve success.

- **Compete culture (market culture)**: These are result-oriented organizations, which focus more on setting targets and deadlines and then delivering. The goal is to dominate markets by whatever means. Employees are encouraged to be competitive with each other, trump their rivals, and keep the organization on top of the competition. Leaders of these types of organizations have high expectations and can be direct, demanding, and driven by success. Needless to say, these organizations will always focus on improving the customer experience and ensuring that their application performs at its best. Amazon and Apple are very good examples of this type of organization, which has a very demanding working environment and strives to achieve and maintain dominance and the edge in all market segments they operate in.

The preceding four categories have been presented in a figure so it's easy to digest:

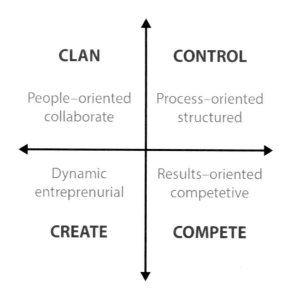

Figure 6.1 – Organization cultures overview

> **Important note**
>
> An organization will always have one trait that is reflected in more than the average number of teams. However, there will be a few teams that will follow a totally different culture, and that is largely because of the leaders in that team. This mix of cultures is a complex topic and is out of the scope of this book.

In all the preceding types of organizations, observability can play an important role in enhancing the efficiency of the organizations and the services it provides. However, since the style of functioning of all these organizations is different, the method of implementation and structures required for the implementation will also be different. You could easily assume that an organization with a **create culture** would be ideal for observability; this type of company can easily adopt new concepts and techniques easily and they thrive on encouraging people to try new things. This doesn't mean the other types of organizations cannot implement observability. We will discuss Observability case study for each type of culture in *Chapter 10, Kickstarting Your Own Observability Journey*. The most important traits to look for in all these organizations are focus on technology, driving technology adoption to make decisions, technology awareness, and openness to try and implement new concepts and methods. If your organization fits this description, then regardless of which organization culture category you belong to, observability can be implemented but with different methods of implementation.

After reading this section, if you are still not able to place your organization in a culture container, don't worry – in the next section, we have more fine-grained descriptions of the characteristics of an organization and how they are related to observability.

Assessing and driving the organization's culture

Hoping that you have now identified the culture type for your organization, let's take a look at some of the key characteristics of an organization that can make or break your observability journey. In this section, we're going to cover the typical traits of organizations that quickly adopt observability. If you find yourself not relating to some of the characteristics, spend some time assessing which key benefits of observability might be impacted by their absence. If they are not your priority, you need not worry much about them. If they are your priority in the observability journey, you can explore options such as outsourcing, upskilling existing resources, or driving programs for a cultural shift.

Being data-driven

Why is data becoming so core to modern organizations? According to McKinsey Global Institute, the **data-driven organization** is likely to acquire 23 times more customers, is 6 times more likely to retain customers, and is 19 times more likely to be more profitable. The insights provided by data help the organization to make better decisions, enhance efficiency, and create a better customer experience. Sounds familiar… right? Very similar to outcomes from matured observability environments. We have touched upon these outcomes in almost all chapters of this book. Observability can be considered part of the wider data-driven ecosystem of an organization. While the organization generates data related to various parts of the organization, observability provides a different dimension to this data and provides a more in-depth understanding of its services and related technologies by correlating these datasets, regardless of their velocity and volume. If your organization is already on the path to becoming data-driven, then observability is an easy addition to the strategy.

> **Note**
> Observability should be considered as a part of the organization's data-driven strategy. By adopting this method, the data generated by observability can be fed to the larger data ecosystem, where it can be used and reused multiple times to derive the maximum ROI.

Ensuring data literacy

Most organizations use data to make business decisions. For example, sales volumes, margin per product, demand forecast, and so on are traditional datasets used commonly by businesses to make key decisions. In modern days, organizations can generate data related to all levels of operation, and the same data can be used to make decisions at every level of the organization. For this to happen, the employees of the organization need to be **data-literate**, i.e., able to analyze and deliberate with data, and use it for decision-making at every level. Organizations need to encourage their people to acquire data literacy skills or hire talent with these skills. The organization also needs to encourage employees to be curious about their own data, and data discovery should be made a key component of the day-to-day responsibilities. These will allow the organizations to learn and discover more about the business, services, and underlying technologies. As the volume of data is increasing every day, we need to be able to separate the noise from the data, which is easily achievable via data literacy. We have mentioned earlier in this book that you should always deliberately choose what data you must ingest into the observability tools. This remains true even when you have data-literate people. Separating noise is just one outcome of data literacy; the most important aspect is identifying the data that can be analyzed to produce the desired results. Feeding this data into observability tools will drive a good-quality observability implementation.

> **Note**
>
> In a nutshell, data literacy is not an outcome of observability, its a driver for a mature and successful observability implementation. Teams with more data literate members will aid in creating high quality, high value data by eliminating noise and enriching the data on a continuous basis.

Providing executive endorsement

As mentioned earlier, implementing observability is not just about technology but also about changing the culture of the organization. Driving a cultural change can include the items in this non-exhaustive list, which often require an executive endorsement to flourish:

- Consistent endorsement and championing of observability and its benefits for executives from faster adoption

- Investment in the right tools and resources

- Hiring skills-based talent such as people with exposure to new technologies, data literacy, and so on, rather than hiring for a narrow role

- Encouraging employees to make decisions based on data and ensuring that data is accessible to everyone transparently

- Improving processes to include automation to reduce human error and gain agility

- Building a safe environment where teams can openly exchange ideas to promote application correlation
- Prioritizing customer experience over everything

Our list is based on the most important factors that are needed for materializing the benefits of Observability listed in the previous section.

Executives can particularly focus on evangelizing observability as capital, committing resources for observability-related solutions, embedding data literacy and advocacy as part of the business goals, and aiding the changes to procurement, hiring, and governance processes for achieving observability-related goals.

Establishing a governance model

All organizations need a **governance model** and related processes to exercise oversight over the organization and its activities. A governance model is a set of practices that includes processes, standards, compliance with regulations, reporting and monitoring, audit-related rules, ethical standards, and so on. These governance practices help the organization set rules, enforce standards, and drive the organization to achieve specific goals or targets. A typical large organization with multiple teams, applications, domains, and even geographical locations can result in people working in isolation. This will eventually result in creating islands of data, observability and monitoring tools galore, and inconsistent standards and processes for managing data required for observability. This will impede the collaboration between teams and limit data sharing across the organization, both of which are the foundations for becoming an end-to-end observable organization.

The following are a few governance practices that need to be implemented and/or enhanced to help drive observability.

Architecture forum

Architecture forums are working groups set up within an organization, generally comprising the enterprise architects, where they discuss, debate, and decide on major technology decisions, concepts and roadmaps to drive efficiencies, technology adoption, implement new standards, and so on. This is the forum where all the projects go for technology approvals. Once submitted, architects review the design and validate whether the design complies with the organization's architectural principles and standards. Hence, for observability, this forum is the key to propagating, evangelizing, and even mandating the observability principle to be considered in every technology decision that is made. Observability becomes another standard or framework that all the projects or teams need to adhere to, and the architecture forum can ensure these frameworks are implemented consistently across the organization.

Data governance

As an organization generates more and more data, governance of the data is becoming critical to ensure data is generated, collected, managed, and used efficiently and appropriately; data quality is improved; and data security and compliance are maintained. The urgency of **data governance** has been increasing exponentially due to the increased digitalization of services, increased cloud adoption, and the implementation of new data privacy regulations across countries. A data governance program can comprise a data governance team, a governance forum, and possibly data engineers to help, advise, and consult the wider organization. The governance team can contribute and work with the observability team and architecture forum to create an observability framework and standards, as they can provide guidance on data-related regulations to the technical teams. These standards and frameworks then feed into architectural decisions for all applications repeatedly.

Procurement and Sourcing

The **procurement and sourcing** department of an organization is an interesting part of the observability journey. This team is responsible for the sourcing and procurement of technology and managing vendors. This team needs to be sensitized regarding observability and its benefits, as onboarding the right vendors, technologies, and products is key to the success of the observability journey. As an outcome of sensitization, while choosing or reviewing product proposals, the procurement team can focus on features such as the ability to handle large volumes of data from various sources and formats (logs, metrics, and traces), generate alerts and incidents, use machine learning to correlate data, create business views, and so on, which aid in implementing observability. If tools are chosen keeping the above features in mind, it will also be easy to integrate them. If the potential vendor has compatibility with the observability standards of the organization, procurement team can help in negotiating either to include these capabilities in the vendors' product road map or provide these capabilities in the future releases.

Observability team

In simple terms, the **observability team** is a team dedicated to managing observability practices within the organization. They work with enterprise architects to define the observability framework and standards and provide input to the procurement team to select the observability toolset based on the organization's observability strategy. This team develops observability standards and processes, advises organization on observability strategy and implementation, acts as custodian of the observability tools, conducts life cycle management, and so on. This centralized approach helps to ensure consistency in the standards, processes, patterns, and tools used in the organization. It is also very important to make the distinction that the observability team is not responsible for the implementation of observability.

> **Note**
>
> In summary, *the job is not to provide fish but to provide rods, reels, baits, and weather reports so that the people can fish themselves.*

Summary

As we have emphasized many times in this book, for a successful observability implementation, the organization as a whole needs to be prepared: goals need to be reprioritized, new standards and frameworks need to be introduced, new processes need to be created or existing ones to be adapted, employees need to be trained/retrained, and so on.

Analyze the culture of your organization and find out whether it is clan, control, create, or compete. Use the guidance in this chapter to assess the benefits of observability that are easily supported by the culture of your organization. While reading through, you must have made mental notes on whether you are part of a data-driven organization and whether you have data-literate people who can help in analyzing the data collected from various data sources. You will also need a governance model to help you in developing standards and a framework for observability. All this may sound overwhelming but we never said that observability comes easy! Observability need to be designed and built in all the systems and services that the organization has, over a period of time to derive the full benefits.

There is a need to bring significant changes to organizational culture to get the desired quality of observability. The executives play a pivotal role in carefully analyzing the existing organizational structure and ways of working. They must be prepared to invest time and effort and to make necessary organizational changes, in line with the observability goals. Put simply, buying a few observability tools and hiring a few engineers won't cut it.

Achieving and Measuring Observability Success

In this book, we have stated multiple times that observability is about a change in culture within an organization, which results in a change in the way the organization thinks, behaves, and organizes itself. But how do we assess the level of current maturity implementation, how do we start the observability journey keeping a particular maturity level as a goal, what kind of people skills are needed for a maturity level, and how do we measure the progress of this journey?

This chapter provides answers to all these questions in detail as well as guardrails for you to implement the maturity levels in your organization and engage the people with the required skill sets. We believe the observability journey must be treated as any organizational-level change, probably not to the extent of an organizational restructuring, but close to it. Therefore, we need a mechanism to monitor, measure, and report on the progress and success of the journey.

Exploring observability maturity levels

Before embarking on any multi-year transformational journey, we need to decide on the targets and stages that the organization needs to traverse and achieve. In the case of observability, one good way to frame this is by using maturity levels. A maturity level can be defined as a set of characteristics that an application and its respective teams need to demonstrate in its day-to-day operations based on the application's criticality, architecture, technology, and business and operational requirements. For example, *Application A* might be customer-facing, which generates revenue for the organization and hence has a high criticality rating and requires a very high level of maturity compared to *Application B*, which is used internally by staff. *Application B*, which does not have any impact on the customers or services the organization provides, needs only a very basic level of maturity.

As part of the observability frameworks, organizations can create maturity levels that act as logical targets that various application teams must achieve. These characteristics can be measured and reported periodically to track the progress and adoption of observability in the organization. By organizing the maturity in this way, organizations can lay a comprehensive roadmap for their observability journey and drive the application teams to select an appropriate maturity level and achieve it over a period of time. By constantly reporting the application's or service's maturity level, organizations can keep the spotlight on observability across the organization and make sure it is not forgotten as the applications and services evolve.

Initial

At this maturity level, application teams have a very basic level of generic monitoring. Service often works and when outages happen, the support teams struggle to identify the problem and restore the services.

The characteristics of this level of maturity are as follows:

- No observability capability
- Basic monitoring is available for infrastructure and there is no or minimal application-level monitoring
- Monitoring is isolated and there is no sharing of data across the organization
- Very reactive in problem-solving
- An inventory of IT assets is available

Managed

At this maturity level, each application team does have monitoring at the infrastructure and application levels. The Ops team would have implemented a monitoring solution for specific problems and issues.

The characteristics of this level of maturity are as follows:

- Rudimentary application monitoring is available
- Monitoring solutions have been implemented for achieving specific goals and for known issues and problems
- The application support team is generally capable of identifying issues quickly and restoring the services
- Monitoring solutions are isolated and tailored for the individual teams
- An inventory of IT assets is available and is accurate

Defined

At a defined maturity level, the application teams would have started following an organization-wide set of frameworks, practices, and tools. This is also driven by the culture of an organization.

The characteristics of this level of maturity are as follows:

- Application teams have started endorsing and implementing enterprise-wide monitoring frameworks, processes, and tools (e.g., observability framework)

- Common patterns, standard integration methods, industry standard, and so on are defined and endorsed organization- wide, and application teams have started using them

- Emphasis is given to generating data and sharing it with the wider organization to be used by other parts of the organization

- Business-level metrics and end user experience monitoring are used to measure the effectiveness of the services

- The teams have advanced skills in using the enterprise observability tools

- Focus is shifted to service-level end-to-end observability instead of application-level observability

- An accurate inventory of IT assets is available, and business processes are recorded in a centralized location

Quantitatively Managed

At this level, organization and application teams would have implemented processes and best practices in implementing monitoring and observability. Also, processes are put in place to measure the success and the performance of the observability and its continuous adoption and implementation.

The characteristics of this level of maturity are as follows:

- Application teams have institutionalized observability in the life cycle, from the design stage to development, implementation, and operations

- Measures of observability success across various teams are monitored and reported at regular intervals

- Efficient methods and processes are implemented to effectively control and monitor data sharing and protection

- Data integrity and quality are monitored to ensure the accuracy of the observability outcome

- Application teams proactively identify most of the problems before they occur and quickly respond to unplanned events

Optimized

This is the highest maturity level, which will close the loop for observability, where the organizations or application teams start to derive value in terms of monetary benefits. This can be achieved either by generating revenue using the outputs from observability or by reducing the operational cost by optimizing processes or resources.

The characteristics of this level of maturity are as follows:

- Application teams start to actively use the outcome of the observability to drive efficiency, improve sales, improve customer experience, reduce wastage, and so on, which can result in monetary benefits

- Operation teams have mastered the concepts of observability and, by using this, a high level of automation is achieved

- Application teams use observability outcomes to trigger workflows or CI/CD pipelines, which can resolve/mitigate the issues on the fly, augment capacity to manage traffic spikes, preserve user experience, and so on

- Observability outcomes are being used in other wider use cases within the organization such as SecOps, FinOps, etc., there by driving more value from the data

- Optimize the data quantity and quality to a maximum resulting in reduced cost and higher ROI

- Application team members are proficient in observability tools and can hypothesize various concepts and implement them with confidence

In the preceding maturity level, most of the organization will be at the *managed* maturity level, where there will be some amount of isolated monitoring at the infrastructure and application levels. There is no focus on sharing information or the concept of end-to-end service-level monitoring. The aim is to nudge and encourage teams to achieve *Defined* and *Quantitatively Managed* levels as a must across the organization, and *Optimized* as a maturity level for a carefully selected set of applications and services, as this level is quite hard to achieve, is difficult to maintain, and will incur a cost. Hence, this will be appropriate for mission-critical applications and services.

People are an important aspect of the success of observability implementation, so in the next section, we will take you through the set of skills that will help you build the right team to achieve the required observability proficiency.

Understanding people and skills

We have referred to people and skills many times and even mentioned them briefly in *Chapter 3*, as both are required for successful observability implementations. It's a common misconception that to set up observability, all one needs is a skilled observability team. That is only a half-truth. Since the application teams are responsible for developing and maintaining the application, there are certain skills that application teams must have to make observability implementation a success. We cannot reiterate enough that the observability team is just a facilitator, but the actual adoption and implementation are the applications team's responsibility. Hence, the observability skills of the application teams are critical.

In this section, we will deep dive into the skills that the application team and observability team should look out for when setting up observability in the organization. The choice of skills will also be guided by the maturity levels discussed earlier. Implementing observability effectively requires a combination of technical and non-technical skills. In our view, here are some of the key skills required to implement observability.

Technical skills

In this section, we will discuss the skills required to perform observability-specific tasks. Some skills require just a deep understanding of the theoretical and practical aspects of a particular technology, tool, or technique, while some others require the ability to apply that knowledge to solve problems and accomplish goals.

In the observability space, technical skills are essential for both application and observability teams.

Application teams

Let's first discuss some broadly scoped technical skills required by the application teams. In the context of your organization, you may need to add a few more to the list, and some from the following list may not be relevant to you:

- **Knowledge of underlying infrastructure**: Understanding the infrastructure and architecture of the application system is essential for effective observability. The application team should know about the infrastructure they operate on, whether it's the cloud, Kubernetes, mainframe, or database. Understanding cloud platforms such as AWS, Google Cloud, or Azure is important for setting up and managing observability solutions in a cloud environment. The entire team should possess this understanding, ranging from basic to proficient level, where the engineers and developers can understand how to build and operate applications effectively in the chosen infrastructure.

- **Observability concepts**: The application team members and stewards must understand observability at a conceptual level so that the developers and engineers can internalize the already defined observability framework and standards and drive its adoption, develop signals, or generate data required for measuring application health or identifying issues. For example, Google Golden Signal (explained in *Chapter 2*) must be internalized, and corresponding metrics need to be identified for the implementation.

- **Instrumentation capability**: Knowledge and/or sound understanding of the relevant programming languages in which the application is coded can be quite helpful, while instrumenting applications to produce the required logs, metrics, and traces for enabling observability.

- **Proficient in Observability Tools**: Observability teams can help in implementing and configuring the enterprise observability tools. However, the application team must have the knowledge and skills to effectively use these tools on a day-to-day basis. If the operations engineers are lacking these skills, then sufficient training is to be provided to upskill them. In our experience, teams that have engineers with a high level of skills in the tools tend to use the capability more and have a better chance and motivation to move to a higher maturity level.

- **Knowledge of open source standards**: Some of the most interesting developments in observability are happening in the open source world. As discussed in *Chapter 9*, the open source community is driving the establishment of new observability standards and practices, such as OpenTelemetry, OpenTracing, and so on. Developers and architects should keep abreast of these developments and explore every opportunity to adopt these standards in consultation with the observability team.

- **Continuous learning mindset**: Keeping up with new technologies, best practices, and industry trends is important for staying current and ensuring that observability practices are effective and relevant.

- **Machine learning concepts**: Machine learning is becoming increasingly important in observability as it can help engineers gain insights into complex distributed systems, which would be difficult or impossible to achieve using traditional monitoring and analysis techniques. The most common application is anomaly detection and predicting future system behavior. So, familiarity with machine learning concepts is a good skill for application teams. Most observability tools have machine learning capabilities that are either enabled by default or configured and fine-tuned by the observability team. Machine learning concepts are more relevant to the teams which have achieved higher maturity level.

Observability team

Let's now take a look at the technical skills required by the observability team. Take note that while there is an overlap with the technical skills required for the application team, the level of proficiency differs. Refer to this section while writing up job descriptions for the observability-related roles in your team:

- **Deep knowledge of monitoring and logging tools**: Expert-level knowledge of tools is crucial for implementing observability. We recommend hiring at least one expert per tool used in the organization. For references on tools, refer to *Chapter 9*.

- **Familiarity with programming languages**: These skills become critical if the organization chooses open source tools, as deep technical skills are required for the development, implementation, and operation of open source tools. If the organization chooses vendor-developed tools, having these skills in the teams will help immensely during instrumentation, developing new integration patterns, integrating tools to downstream systems for automation, and so on.

- **Ability to understand system architecture**: A good understanding of system architecture is essential for designing and implementing an observability solution. This includes knowledge of distributed systems, microservices architecture, and containerization.

- **Infrastructure knowledge**: Observability engineers should have the skills to work with the infrastructure engineers to create and maintain patterns and standards for the observability framework and for the application engineers to consume.

- **Strong understanding of metrics, logs, and traces**: This is essential for configuring the dashboards, alerts, incidents, and other knowledge artifacts on the observability tools. This also includes a thorough knowledge of data collection, storage, and analysis.

- **Data analysis**: An interest in data analysis and a good understanding of statistical analysis and data visualization is essential for making sense of the large amounts of data generated by an observability solution.

Communication skills

Technical skills will get the implementation done, but observability programs require a continuous dialog between the application and observability teams to enable data ingestion, dashboards, alerts, data correlation, data analysis, and many more related tasks. Any change or downtime on either side can have an impact on both teams, which needs to be communicated, and both teams need to collaborate to get through the situation or to achieve any planned goals. So, the following communication skills are important for both teams:

- **Effective communication skills**: These are important for effectively communicating the value and benefits of observability to stakeholders, as well as for communicating any issues or concerns that arise.

- **Consulting and collaboration skills**: As observability engineers need to work across the organization with multiple teams, consulting and collaboration skills will be extremely useful in meeting the challenges in such a diverse environment. Application teams also benefit from these skills, as engineers will be able to work effectively with other enabling teams such as infrastructure teams, architects, developers, and so on for observability implementation. For end-to-end service-level observability, these skills become critical, as the kind of collaboration required will stretch across multiple application teams and their engineers, developers, and architects.

Problem-solving skills

One major goal of observability is to reduce the number of incidents or avert them altogether, allowing teams to take timely action. To achieve this goal, both application and observability teams should have the following problem-solving skills:

- **Analytical skills**: Analytical skills are important for identifying and resolving issues in the system being monitored

- **Troubleshooting skills**: Troubleshooting skills are important for effectively diagnosing and resolving issues that arise

Any team with a combination of these skills is considered well equipped to implement observability successfully. This team can then work together to effectively implement observability practices and ensure that the organization can make the most of the benefits that observability provides.

Mapping skills and maturity levels

We have discussed the maturity levels and the typical skills required by the application team and observability team. Once you have made a decision on the maturity level for your organization, use the following mapping to understand the skills required to achieve that level. Kindly note that you may need to adjust the mapping in the context of any organization-specific skills.

You may use this legend to read *Table 7.1*:

	Basic
	Intermediate
	Advanced
	Not Applicable

The following table covers the skills of the application teams only, as the observability teams must have all the skills at all levels of maturity:

Skills	Initial	Managed	Defined	Quantitatively Managed	Optimized
Knowledge of underlying infrastructure					
Observability concepts					
Instrumentation capability					
Proficient in Observability Tools					
Knowledge of open source standards					
Continuous learning mindset		Basic	Intermediate	Advanced	
Machine learning concepts					
Effective communication skills					
Collaboration skills					
Analytical skills		Basic	Intermediate	Advanced	
Troubleshooting skills					

Table 7.1 – Maturity levels and people skills mapping

Using the skills and the table mapping the skills to the observability maturity levels, you can work toward building the right team for the targeted maturity level. Keep in mind that there is also an option to upskill existing resources. Hence, in the next section, let us discuss how observability can be measured using some defined metrics.

Measuring observability

Implementing observability is a multi-year journey that includes accurately reporting how much progress has been made and reporting to the business how far they are in the journey. It also provides an opportunity to benchmark the progress of each team in relation to the rest of the organization; this can be a very motivating and inspiring attribute. These measures will help the engineers and developers to keep the focus on observability and encourage them to slowly acquire and develop the skills required for the observability journey. Let's say that this slowly and surely prompts the positioning of observability at the center of every activity of the teams resulting in a cultural change.

Measuring the success of monitoring practices is essential to understanding the effectiveness of your monitoring strategies and making improvements where necessary. The following key metrics are good indicators of the success of observability implementation. Most of them should apply to all organizations. Feel free to add anything specific to your organization. You can also pick and choose metrics from this list based on your observability goals:

- **Alerts and incident frequency**: These metrics measure the number of known alerts and incidents that occur in a particular period for the organization. A reduction in incident frequency with an increase in alerts (proactive) can indicate that observability practices are helping to prevent issues from occurring in the first place. These metrics can also be applied per application level and compared with the previous incident-occurring timeline to understand whether observability is making a positive impact on the timeline. Recall from *Chapter 5* that incidents refer to outages that are impacting customers are the first sign of any unhealthy applications or services, and alerts can be defined as issues or events that have not caused any customer impact but can in the future.

> **Important note**
> Sometimes, with increased observability coverage, new incidents may start occurring for an application that was earlier undetected. So, use this metric with caution.

- **Mean time to detect (MTTD)**: This metric measures the time it takes for the observability tools to detect and resolve issues in the production environment. A reduction in time can indicate that observability practices are becoming more effective and are improving incident response times. These times can easily be picked from the incident management tools.

- **Mean time to recovery (MTTR)**: This metric measures the average time it takes to recover from an incident. A reduction in MTTR can indicate that observability practices are helping to identify and resolve issues quickly and efficiently once they have been detected. Again, the time can easily be picked from the incident management tools, irrespective of the tool being used in your organization.

- **Root cause analysis (RCA) accuracy**: This metric measures the accuracy of **RCA** performed during incident response. An increase in RCA accuracy can indicate that observability practices are helping to identify the root cause of issues more quickly and accurately. If this metric is not improving, focus on data collection and alerts that have been put in place for different applications.

- **Lead time for changes**: This metric measures the time from when a change is initiated to when it is deployed to production. A reduction in lead time for changes can indicate that the observability implementation is helping to accelerate the development and deployment process. Part of this metric also measures the percentage of changes that result in failure. Data required for this metric will be available in the tool used for raising change records.

- **Application deployment cycle**: This metric measures the time it takes to go from code change to deployment in production. A reduction in cycle time can indicate that observability practices are helping to improve the speed and efficiency of the software development cycles and deployment process. Data for this metric can be gathered from the CI/CD tools or build tools being used in the organization. If this metric is not improving, focus on improving development practices, the quality of deliverables, requirement gathering, and the approval process. (Note: this is an advanced metric, and elementary implementations can skip it if they like.)

- **False-positive error rate**: This metric measures the number of false alarms generated by the monitoring system. A decrease in the false-positive rate can indicate that monitoring practices are becoming more effective at distinguishing between real issues and false alarms.

- **Data quality**: Observability is based on the data generated by the applications. The outcomes of the observability (such as dashboards, alerts, predictions, etc.) will be dependent on the data these tools consume. Hence, measuring the accuracy of the data will help in maintaining the integrity of the observability outcomes. The measure should include metrics such as accuracy, completeness, consistency, timeliness, and any other metrics specific to the technology stack.

- **User review ratings**: This metric measures the level of satisfaction of end users or customers with the system's availability and performance. An increase in user satisfaction can indicate that observability practices are helping to deliver a better user experience. This metric shows progress over time; continue to measure it till you get the desired level.

- **Adoption rate of observability tools**: This metric measures the percentage of users who are engaged with the observability tools. This can be easily captured by looking at unique users per tool. A high adoption rate can indicate that the observability practices have been well received and are being effectively implemented.

Most of these metrics apply to maturity levels starting at *Defined* and going up to *Optimized*. Only a few metrics (such as MTTR, MTTD, and incident frequency) may apply at the *Managed* and *Initial* maturity levels, depending upon the monitoring and observability setup. In most cases, there is not enough data to calculate the metrics at the *Initial* level.

You can regularly monitor and analyze these metrics to measure and understand the success of the observability implementation after it has been implemented. It will help you identify what you are doing well, and which areas need improvement. You can also include them in the initial plan when you propose the observability plan to the leadership team. They would like to know how the outcome of all the spending will be measured and tracked.

Summary

The maturity levels discussed in this chapter will help you to assess your current observability maturity level and also to start your observability journey with a fixed goal. Whether you choose the *initial, defined, managed, quantitatively managed,* or *optimized level,* we have added sufficient guardrails in this chapter for you. Remember, cultural change within the organization requires changes to the values and skills of the people. This chapter intended to emphasize the skills required by the organization, particularly the application team, for this cultural shift.

Along with maturity levels and people skills, this chapter also discussed the importance of measuring the progress of the observability journey, not only to track the progress but also to motivate and reiterate the observability values within the workforce.

8
Identifying the Stakeholders

In this chapter, we will discuss a very important aspect of planning observability for the success of your organization. It is not a technical concept, but it is important to understand as it helps you identify the project goals and requirements, influence, educate and empower the key players, and finally implement an effective communication plan to sustain a long lasting change. And believe us, that is half the work done. If you decide to jump into the thick of things – that is, **implementing** an observability use case that someone read online or has a notion that this particular problem can be solved with observability, or after attending a sleek sales presentation from a vendor – take a step back and identify your stakeholders. Use this chapter as inspiration to do so and, in our experience, the outcome will be of better quality. If your observability use case and implementation are of a *check-the-box* nature, it will be difficult to implement the concepts discussed in this chapter as they are more suited to more structured or large-scale implementations.

In this chapter, we'll understand the roles of the various stakeholders involved in the observability journey. We will be discussing the **drivers**, **users**, **actors**, and **supporters** of observability. Each of them has a unique role and all of them are crucial to the success of the observability implementation. To learn more about each of them, keep reading further.

Enhancement drivers of an organization

As we have emphasized in previous chapters, it is one thing to implement observability and another to maintain it. It is analogous to a house plant. Bringing home a plant and putting it in a pot is not the best use of the plant; it has to be watered, fertilized, pruned as per seasons, and repotted over time. The success of such long-term observability implementations is largely affected by organizations and their cultures, as discussed in *Chapter 6* and *Chapter 7*. Such implementations need constant enhancements as per the demands of the organization. To achieve this, certain drivers need to be put in place.

Engineers and architects can implement an idea that yields technical and business benefits but its adoption across the organization is the responsibility of **leadership**. Many times, it needs grit and constant push as most teams do not like change or stepping out of their comfort zone. The value of the implementation has to be constantly repeated in various forums and tweaked to suit the needs of the teams. In other words, you has to be open to feedback because the team that implements observability is not the only user of it. That brings us to another challenge frequently faced in organizations. Many teams set forth to implement observability where they are the owners and consumers as well. We call those implementations focused use case solving; it's not a practice that can thrive. For enterprise-grade and organization-wide observability implementations, existing monitoring teams or a new team that has monitoring experience should pick up the task. We will talk about this more in the *The actors of observability* section of this chapter.

Let's circle back to the role of leadership in observability adoption. We touched on it in *Chapter 1* and *Chapter 7* when talking about the challenges of implementing observability and discussing the culture of organizations. Leadership teams can be bucketed into five different types – **innovators, early adopters**, **early majority**, **late majority**, and **laggards**. The first two types put in the most amount of hard work and carve the way for the remaining ones. We are not saying that the journey is easy for the latter, just that they have some examples to look up to and known challenges to plan for well ahead of time. Like any other technology adoption, observability implementation will also be driven by the leadership team based on their vision and enthusiasm for the changes.

Another major player that drives observability is the **investment** the organization is willing to make in a practice that needs constant fuel and enhancements. The observability tools and the skills needed to utilize them in the best possible way also need significant monetary and time investments. As more and more teams adopt the observability implementation, the infrastructure will need to be scaled, feedback will increase, and implementing it will often take priority over new enhancements unless the team is large enough to cater to both. Again, as ideal as it sounds, it needs considerable investments.

One factor that's largely overlooked in the adoption of technology is how to maintain people's **motivation** to acquire new skills and work on them. Not everyone likes to learn and come out of their comfort zones. So, plan ahead and identify the numbered few who would be willing to scale up and provide them with robust training or cross-training as needed. Here, you should also engage your technology partners to train your people and discuss case studies that will lead to a clear understanding and new ideas.

The last factor that drives observability is the **vision** of the organization itself. Your technical team may develop a great product and you might also have funds to spare but if the product does not align with the organization's vision, it will soon become a black hole. We do believe in incubation projects, and they are the seed starters for many technical revolutions, but observability has crossed that stage now. You can start small and slow, but it cannot be an incubation project as modern application architectures are constantly becoming complex every day. So, whatever you intend to build, ensure you align it with your organization's vision. Every organization puts a lot of focus on the stability of their systems, low downtimes, and high customer experience, so it should be easy for you to align with this.

When you sit down with your team to plan observability, ensure that you keep leadership informed of the support you would need from them, discuss the availability of funds, and design something in line with the organization's vision.

The actors of observability

Like any initiative, there must be a person or a team that is responsible for observability in an organization. In our experience, especially in a large organization, a centralized monitoring or observability team with the right mandate and endorsement from management should be assigned this task. This helps with standardization, fixing ownership, and being responsible for the overall success of the initiative. This doesn't mean that the observability team is liable for the outcome of the observability process, but for creating the right environment and providing the tools, standards, and processes required by the organization to implement observability via self-service.

Let's return to the analogy of bringing home a plant and expand on it. Consider an office that allows willing employees to keep a plant in the office as part of a green initiative. A team within the organization will make certain decisions to provide some guidelines on how to participate in the initiative. These guidelines are framed to make sure this initiative provides a safe working environment and gauge and limit the effort and time required, so as not to affect productivity. An enthusiastic green-thumbed employee may bring in an endangered plant species that has thorns, which can be a workplace hazard, or another person may bring in a large plant that requires a large pot, needs a lot of watering, and takes up valuable commercial space.

To avoid these scenarios, a team – let's call them the Green Team – establishes guidelines on what kind of plants are allowed, the size and shape of the plants, the types of pots that can be used, the number of plants allowed per person, and so on. To manage the cost, the Green Team can negotiate with a plant nursery for a bulk discount for all the plants, pots, and potting mix used under this initiative. To make the whole process user-friendly, they can set up an internal website from where the employees are allowed to order the plants and pots from the chosen nursery so that the plants are delivered to the office during business hours, thereby limiting the time spent by employees taking part in this initiative and saving valuable productive hours. The employees use the facilities and process set by the Green Team to acquire a plant of their choice from their approved list and follow the guidelines in managing the plants going forward. However, whether the plants survive or thrive depends on the effort and care of the employees themselves. In simple words, the Green Team is not responsible for the outcome of the initiative – they are the facilitators, enablers, and guardians of the initiative.

The same analogy fits observability teams as well. It lays out the standards, processes, and governance structure. The same team can assess various tools in the market, analyze them, and choose one or more tools that are fit for the purpose, negotiate an enterprise-wide bulk license to minimize the cost, and make these tools available for the organization to use.

Now, let's take the green initiative example again. Some of the teams in the organization may decide that one plant per person is not feasible, might be too much effort, they don't have the skills, and so on, and hence the team may adopt a plant or a few plants for the entire team and distribute the responsibilities among the team members. In this scenario, the team members still follow the guidelines framed by the Green Team and organize themselves to participate in the initiative and achieve the outcome, which is to be part of the initiative and take care of a plant in the office. In the same manner, all the team members of an application or business team in an organization may not have all the skills required for the implementation. In such a scenario, the architect or developer, or engineers, can incorporate the observability principle, framework, process, and tools during the design and implementation phase. Once the implementation is done, the application or service can be handed over to the operations teams to manage and maintain. Again, this involves sharing responsibilities among team members across different phases of a project while fully following the **observability framework** laid out by the observability team.

Like any framework or standard, observability also needs regular updates and refinement. The **centralized observability team** can lead the discussion with **enterprise architects**, **enterprise data teams**, and other stakeholders (if required) and make adequate changes to the framework, standards, and processes. This is critical to make the observability implementation fit for purpose and have it adapt to the changes in technology, changes in organizational structure, and regulatory and legislative changes.

Here is a simple and self-explanatory representation to help you visualize how all the different teams and groups, such as the observability team, application team, enterprise architects, and enterprise data teams, come together:

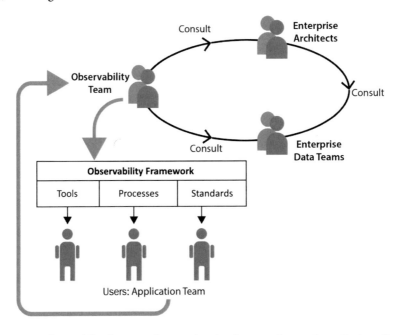

Figure 8.1 – Observability framework – creation, implementation, and practical application

The implementation of observability in an organization requires a responsible team or person, ideally a centralized monitoring or observability team with management support, to standardize and provide the necessary tools, standards, and processes for its successful implementation. Teams across different phases of a project can share responsibilities while following the observability framework laid out by the observability team.

How users prompt improvement

The team that implements enterprise-wide observability is never the team that fully consumes the outcomes of it. It is similar to a central monitoring team that configures existing tools for monitoring the applications in the organization. The configuration that the team performs results in generating alerts that are consumed and acted upon by the owners of that particular application; the same applies to the dashboards. The **observability team** collects feedback from the users and incorporates them into the observability standards and processes. On the other hand, application teams that use and implement the observability in their respective application uses the consumer's feedback for optimizing the observability implementation to improve the outcomes and if required, and advises the observability team for necessary changes in the standards and processes.

Although this seems like a simple explanation, it is one of the trickiest segments in making an observability implementation a success. **Users** (Application Team) have certain responsibilities – they need to evaluate the offering without bias for other products or technology, they need to use it and then provide constructive feedback rather than sharing downright analysis, and they help in promoting the observability implementation by word of mouth, adding credibility. Users are on the receiving end of the implementation and there is no way to control how they will react to the product you present to them:

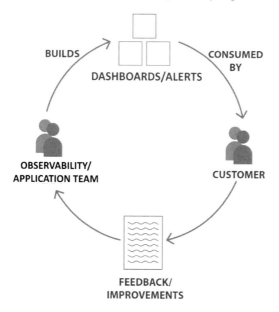

Figure 8.2 – Role of users in the upkeep of observability implementation

For desirable results, along with technology, focus on the process that will impact the users, such as change management for the stability of the platform, the engagement process for easy onboarding, the feedback mechanism, raising bugs, user guides, and more. Any world-class product can fall flat if ease of use for the customers is not baked into the product design. We are not saying that you should design only for the user; just keep in mind that the end user's observability is a huge change that requires work from their end too. If they find the whole process too tedious, there is always a risk that they may not even use it!

Depending on your observability implementation, users may need to instrumentalize their applications to produce the required data, open up the services/ports for external access, scale infrastructure or lambdas to support the data needs, make several changes to the way their applications currently produce logs, review and update their CMDB, or do something highly specific to your organization. It's a huge task. You will need to make it better for your users by letting them know in advance of the changes that you expect of them and the gradual benefits that they will reap from the effort.

Exploring the supporters of observability

Who can support an observability implementation? The short answer is anyone who is going to benefit from it. This ranges from the technology teams who will benefit from increased stability and understanding the complex infrastructure, as well as reduced operating costs, to operations teams who are going to benefit from the reduced mean time to detect/repair, reduced alert fatigue, and more. The business gets insights into how the services are operating and uses these insights to increase the customer experience, thereby advancing the business offering. That's pretty much most of the organization. What we are going to do is suggest a few more very interesting groups of people who can help and support you in the observability journey.

Enterprise architects

As mentioned in *Chapter 7*, the observability team has to work with **enterprise architects** in the organization to standardize the observability framework and ensure the alignment of the observability strategy across the organization. They are responsible for incorporating observability principles and processes in the architectural approval process for the projects and initiatives across the organization. The architect and architecture teams are mandated to align the technology roadmap, create technology coherence, and maximize the use of the existing tools and technology stack. They will be very keen to advise and encourage the **application teams** to follow the observability principles and framework in the design phase itself. This helps in avoiding last-minute design decisions and design changes resulting from afterthoughts.

Enterprise data team

Depending on the type and scale of the organization, your organization may have an **enterprise data team**, which looks after the data management and data handling policies within the organization. If you don't have a dedicated team for this, this function will be handled by some other team, most likely by the architects themselves. As mentioned in *Chapter 2* (while discussing logs, metrics, and traces), mature observability implementation requires generating, collecting, and processing vast amounts of data. Since generating the right amount of data or producing the right insights from this data is quite difficult, data teams will have a vested interest in exploring ways to generate the right data at the right level and explore ways to reuse already collected data for purposes outside observability use cases. This can help avoid data duplication, encourage data sharing, and in the democratization of data across the organization. Hence, it's always advisable to involve and engage the group of people doing this function to understand and align strategies to implement the best practices for data management. This is particularly important as data and its security is a very sensitive topic, and rightly so. Inputs from this team should be part of the observability framework and can generally help in defining the type of data that can be collected from a given source, as well as the data retention and disposal guidelines, how the data can be stored and in which location, and the process and controls that need to be implemented for the protection and optimal use of the collected data. Data related to customers or employees, handling data in and from the cloud, and encryption methodologies are a few common areas that the data team can advise you on.

Sourcing team

The **sourcing team** is a very unusual inclusion in the list of supporters for observability; however, we believe it has a very important role. The primary role of a sourcing team is to source technologies and products for the organization based on the product or service roadmap. Now, consider an organization that mostly depends on off-the-shelf products from vendors to build the technology stacks that provide services to the customers. Since there is no in-house development happening, the scope of the engineers to build observability will be solely dependent on the ability of the off-the-shelf product and/or the vendor that the organization engages. This is where the sourcing team can help. Observability capabilities, the ability to generate and share data, and compatibility with the chosen observability tools and the process should be added as key criteria for the product or vendor selection. In our professional experience, the deficiency of the technology products used has been a source of frustration for observability implementation. For example, network appliances and storage devices have been difficult to extract data from, and the available capabilities were quite rudimentary. SaaS offerings can be challenging, as some vendors do not share any information related to service health other than a plain availability matrix for SLA reporting. The non-availability of the right information at the right depth will create gaps in the observability view. The sourcing team can help in avoiding these products and vendors or can negotiate a commercial arrangement to include observability aspects in their commercial contracts.

Compliance and regulatory teams

This may not apply to a lot of organizations, but for industries that are governed by a lot of legislation and regulatory oversight, **compliance and regulatory teams** can be a source of great support. Banking and financial services, insurance, and payments are good examples of sectors where compliance and regulatory teams play a crucial role in keeping the organization compliant. The compliance teams must periodically report on the performance of various products and services to regulatory organizations, such as central banks, competition commissions, finance commissions, and so on. In some cases, the performance metrics of some of the services need to be provided on a near real-time basis to customers and competitors by law. In these scenarios, observability can be implemented in the relevant product and service technology stacks, with a focus on specific outcomes to satisfy compliance requirements. From our experience, these compliance requirements have single-handedly justified the implementation of observability and its cost. In some cases, this resulted in refreshing the entire technology stack and implementing observability to achieve regulatory compliance.

Introducing the RASCI matrix

So far, we have discussed the drivers, users, actors, and supporters, each in their own context. Throughout this book, we have been talking about which team is responsible for what type of actions. You might have made mental notes of it. To make things easier, we can use the **RASCI matrix (R = Responsible, A = Accountable, S = Support, C = Consulted, I = Informed)**, which is a standard method for representing the roles of various stakeholders of a project.

The following table provides a high-level summary of the RASCI matrix for observability implementation:

Tasks	Set the Vision	Observability Framework	Tools and Processes	Governance	Observability Implementation
Management	Accountable Responsible	Informed	Support	Informed	Informed
Observability team	Supports	Accountable Responsible	Responsible Accountable (not always)	Accountable	Support
Enterprise architects	Informed	Consulted Support	Consulted	Accountable	Support
Enterprise data team	Support	Consulted		Consulted	
Regulatory and compliance team		Consulted		Consulted	
Sourcing team		Consulted	Consulted		
Application teams	Informed	Informed	Informed	Informed	Accountable

Table 8.1 – RASCI matrix for observability

You can apply this RASCI matrix as is or make certain changes to it, depending on how the involved teams are set up in your organization. For example, the enterprise data team and enterprise architects may be a single unit performing both functions, so you should merge the rows for them so that you can reach out to them at appropriate times.

Summary

In simple terms, to successfully implement observability, different parts of the organization must work toward a single vision. Management must evangelize this vision and encourage and empower various stakeholders and actors to make changes to their processes and ways of working to aid this observability journey. Each of these stakeholders directly or indirectly contributes to or actively participates in its implementation and/or governance. How well these stakeholders perform and cooperate will ultimately dictate the success of observability.

In this chapter, we provided descriptions of drivers, users, actors, and supporters. We also gave you a RASCI matrix to help you understand how all these stakeholders work together. You may or may not be able to neatly identify them in your organization initially, but keep them in mind while planning your observability implementation. Having the right teams and people on your observability journey can have a significant impact on the quality of the outcome.

9

Deciding the Tools for Observability

We hope that you enjoyed reading about the drivers, users, actors, and supporters of observability. It is a stream that often gets overlooked but it is key for planning good-quality observability. The involvement of the right teams and building for the right customer can make a significant difference in the quality of the outcome.

This chapter focuses on something we have been talking about throughout this book – observability **toolsets**! We will provide you with the guardrails for choosing a tool in the context of your business needs and organizational culture. We will also drop in some advice on whether you should buy new tooling, build it on your own, or leverage the existing toolsets that you already have. To bring everything together from the previous chapters, we will share references for tools for specific types of monitoring. Since we will be discussing some observability case studies in the next chapter, we will also discuss the future of observability and the role of OpenTelemetry in implementing it.

Developing a strategy

The objective of an observability tool is to analyze the data generated by applications and provide meaningful insights that can either improve the performance of the services or prevent outages and service disruptions. A carefully drafted **tools strategy** will provide an organization with a centralized platform or a set of compatible tools that can work with all the technology stacks used by the organization, as well as its operational framework. The tool strategy also needs to identify the functions and features that are required by the organization.

As part of creating the tool strategy, the first question that needs to be answered will be what kind of tool sets are required to achieve the objectives. This is primarily driven by the size, scale, and diversity of technologies used by the organization. An organization that is using more diverse technologies may require more than one tool or analytic solution compared to a monolithic organization that concentrates on a few services. An example would be a financial institution compared to an online store. A financial institution offers multiple services, such as normal day-to-day banking, home loans, ATM services, insurance services, and more, and these services may be hosted in on-premise data centers to the cloud, while an online store will have a few services related to online purchases. Hence, the technology stack of a financial institution can be very complex compared to an online store. We recommend concentrating on the following two strategies:

- **Monolithic strategy**: The monolithic strategy is primarily suitable for organizations with more or less monolithic technology stacks. As described earlier, an online store can run the entire service in the cloud using microservices. In such a scenario, what the organization requires is a tool or a platform that can work very well as a container platform and provide observability to the underlying infrastructure, applications stack, and end user layers. The advantage of this strategy is that the organization will likely have a single centralized tool and streamlined adoption methods. Since the observability framework, observability onboarding and operational process, and more are standardized, with less overhead for training, the developers, operational support engineers, users, and others will find the observability journey less complex, easier, and more enjoyable. The disadvantage is that this won't work in an environment that has diverse technology stacks.

- **Tool kits strategy**: A large organization such as a financial institution will have a large and diverse technology stack and its infrastructure and services will be spread across its data centers, the cloud, and SaaS. It may also have a legacy infrastructure, appliances, network devices, and outsourced managed services. In such an environment, having one tool that's compatible with all types of technology stacks, to satisfy all the requirements, will be difficult. In this case, a set of tools or a tool kit may be required. Hence, the priority should be to choose a limited set of tools that are compatible with each other, can work together, and can share data as well. There should also be a focus on reducing the number of tools as much as possible to prevent **data islands** and concentrate on the synergy of the selected tools. The synergy of these tools doesn't mean buying different types of tools from the same vendor – it simply means each tool can interact and integrate at ease to provide an outcome. This method can satisfy the diverse set of requirements and the technology stack across the organization and also allow you to have specialized tools for a particular technology product without compromising the overall observability objective. The disadvantage is that since multiple tools are used, synergy may not be possible for all the use cases and requirements. Multiple tools will require multiple onboarding methods, operation processes, and training requirements. The developers, operational support engineers, and users may find the whole observability suite challenging and complex. The success of this strategy will depend on the level of synergy between the selected tool and the ability of the organization to address the observability challenges, as described in *Chapter 3* in the *Challenges faced by organizations in the real world* section.

Once you have decided on a tools strategy that's suitable for your organization, the next step is to look for the tools that will work the best for you. There are several options available in the market and many of them have overlapping functions, which can make choosing the right tool very difficult. So, in the next section, we will take you through some features that the observability tools must have for a successful observability implementation.

Desirable features of observability tools

As part of the tool strategy or tool selection process, the organization must agree and decide on the requirements for the tool. These requirements should be based on the organization's business, technological, and operational needs, as well as its goals. How the tool(s) are going to be used, the users of the tools, the depth of technical knowledge of the staff, the future technology roadmap, and more are very good questions to be addressed while assessing the tools. In the following sections, we will discuss a few desirable features that observability tools should have.

Well-developed integration patterns

We already know that observability requires a lot of data, and all this data needs to be extracted from the systems and services by the tool, or the systems themselves require the data to be forwarded to the observability tool. Different technology stacks and infrastructure platforms will have different set of complexities and challenges, hence requiring different capabilities or integration patterns. A good observability tool will have a predefined, well-developed integration pattern that can be used to seamlessly integrate with different technologies with minimal configuration or code changes. Some of the common integrations that you should look for are integration with cloud platforms and workloads, container platforms, different OS types, databases, network devices, external systems like ticketing systems, notification solutions, and so on. This ease of integration will help in driving the adoption of observability and provide a better and faster return on investment without many disruptions to services.

Standard dashboards and customization potential

For a great user experience, the observability tool should have a ready-to-use, off-the-shelf standard set of dashboards and/or alerts based on the technology stacks that are being monitored. These dashboards or alerts can be a quick and easy way to unlock value and can be based on generic use cases. The tool should provide engineers with the option to customize these dashboards to their requirements based on the technology implementation in the respective organizations. Standard dashboards enable observability teams to provide an immediate outcome to the users while the users are figuring out how to optimize the dashboard so that it's suitable for their operational and business needs.

Support of configuration as code

Configuration as Code (CaC) involves defining the configuration of a system/application/tool in a programming language or a structured format, such as YAML or JSON. These configuration files can be version controlled, tested, and deployed in a similar way to application code. While this may feel *nice to have* in the beginning for observability tools, with time, as the system scales and teams change hands, CaC comes in very handy for replicating configurations across different environments, automating configuration management, reducing human errors, and improving consistency across environments. With these features, CaC makes it easier to scale observability tools to handle larger systems or more complex environments.

Ease of use

Data has started to play a very important role in modern-day organizations, and analytic and observability tools have democratized this data so that it can be accessed and used by a wider audience. However, to enable different users and stakeholders across the organization to use the data effectively, the ease of use of the tool is very critical. Vendors are now giving great importance to designing easy-to-use interfaces and making the tool user-friendly to users with various levels of skills. One of the interesting ways to assess these tools for ease of use is to select a few people representing the cross-section of the users in your organization – such as an engineer, support engineer, and a business analyst – and provide access to an observability tool, where an application or service has been already onboarded. Provide them with a suitable amount of time and ask them to summarize what they learned about the application and service by using the tool. The more a user can learn from using the tool without much context, the better the tool design is. Even though this is a very rudimentary approach, this can provide an accurate assessment of the tool's ease of use. A well-designed tool will reduce the technical knowledge required to use the tool and hence require less training, thereby driving the adoption at all levels of the organization.

Granular access control

Observability tools collect data from multiple sources. Some portions of this data may be readable on a need-only basis or have restrictions on who can access it. So, granular access control is important for observability tools because it allows organizations to control who can access sensitive data and ensure that only authorized personnel have access to critical information.

The purpose of observability tools is to provide insights into the performance, behavior, and health of complex applications, which may include sensitive data such as user information, transaction details, and system logs. Without granular access control, any user with access to an observability tool would be able to view all the data it collects, including sensitive information that they may not be authorized to see. This could lead to unauthorized access, data breaches, and potential legal and regulatory compliance issues.

Granular access control allows organizations to define roles and permissions for different users and groups, which can be tailored to specific datasets and types of information. For example, a company might create different access levels for developers, testers, and production support teams, with different permissions for viewing, editing, and deleting data. By implementing granular access control, observability tools can provide visibility into complex systems while ensuring that sensitive data remains protected. This enhances data security and promotes better compliance with data privacy regulations, such as GDPR, CCPA, and HIPAA. Consider this feature with great weightage if the observability tool in your organization is expected to handle any kind of sensitive data. In general, all tools support limiting data access based on user roles and permissions – you need to pay special attention to support for specific data compliances that apply to your organization.

Supporting multiple tenancies

From an organization-wide observability implementation perspective, the ability of the tool to support multiple tenancies has tremendous value. As we have mentioned previously, in a large organization, the observability team should provide tools, processes, and frameworks for the engineers and users to consume. By providing them with adequate training and best practice guidelines, developers and engineers are empowered and encouraged to self-serve the tools and implement the observability framework themselves. Since application teams themselves know the application well and the data it generates, with the right amount of training and support, these engineers and developers can become masters of their destiny. To facilitate this, the observability tool should be able to support multiple tenancies where the engineers and developers from these application teams (tenants) can build, test, modify, and maintain configurations without impacting other tenants or applications, with limited or no support from the observability team. This is the only practical way to drive adoption across the organization at scale. Failure to do so will result in a bottleneck for observability implementation; the centralized observability team will be the only team with the skills and elevated access to perform the associated tasks, which will create an unnecessary critical dependency.

Data sharing and external integration

An application has implemented observability and built dashboards and alerts for its different stakeholders who are using the capability daily. How do we further extend the value of the tool and the data it holds? One way is to allow users to reuse the same data, multiple times in multiple ways. For that, the data that has been generated and stored by the observability tools should be able to be shared with other tools or platforms. This data can be shared in a raw or in abstract format – whichever suits the use case. Another way to enhance this value is to allow the observability tools to be integrated with other downstream systems so that the outcomes from the tool can be used to drive further outcomes outside the tools. For example, alerts generated by the tools can be fed to a notification solution to notify the stakeholder or a self-healing solution to automate the process of recovery in case of a service outage. Other interesting external integration examples are capacity management tools or cost management and transparency tools, where observability data can enrich and enhance these tools' capabilities. The focus should be to reuse the data for various use cases, drive multiple outcomes, and unlock value by integrating it into many downstream systems.

Implementation of data science techniques

Nowadays, every vendor has **data science** as part of their product portfolio. The same is true for observability tools. A good implementation of data science, for a real-world use case, is very challenging as the users should know how, when, and which algorithms can be used for which scenarios. Hence, the availability of a pre-packaged set of algorithms for predefined, well-developed use cases can be very empowering for the users of observability. This will allow users to enjoy the benefits of data science without delving into too much detail. We believe that if the tools allow users to import custom libraries for building and testing models using custom algorithms, it can be advantageous to application or service teams that have developers and engineers with advanced data science skills. These custom capabilities are not a must but are advisable for an organization that has a good data science background.

High availability

Once an observability tool goes live, it starts collecting and maintaining a lot of data from multiple applications to monitor their health and performance. It then uses this data to provide actionable insights to the teams and helps in avoiding costly consequences. So, these tools must have built-in **high availability** (**HA**) to ensure that they remain operational, even in the event of hardware or software failures, and continue to serve their customers, even if one or more of their components fail. If you are building a tool, HA can be achieved by using redundant hardware or software components, load balancing, or failover mechanisms, among other techniques. In addition to improving service quality, HA can also help reduce the impact of maintenance and upgrades. By ensuring that the tool remains available during upgrades or maintenance, observability teams can avoid interruptions to their monitoring and analysis processes, leading to increased operational efficiency and better insights into system behavior. Look out for this feature while choosing observability tools as it provides the required resilience and reliability to maintain visibility into complex systems and applications, even when things go south.

Scalability

Whether you would like to start small and grow later, or you have a clear understanding of your use case and expectations from the observability tool, we still recommend that you consider the scalability feature of the tool while making the decision. Scalability is an important feature for observability tools because as the scale and complexity of the systems that are being monitored grow, the amount of data generated also increases, which can quickly overwhelm a tool that is not designed for scalability. A scalable observability tool can handle large amounts of data and can adapt to the changing needs of an organization. This means that as the volume of data increases, the tool can handle the increased load without sacrificing performance or accuracy. It also means that the tool can accommodate changes in the target system or application, such as introduction of new components, increased traffic, and so on.

Open source adoption

Vendors can lock or limit their products & solutions' features and capabilities for commercial reasons. As the open source community gains acceptance and maturity, it is advised that you select a tool that adopts open source concepts and principles in the technology roadmap. The industry is trying to standardize observability patterns, frameworks, data structures, data collection methods, and, to some extent, processing methods as well. OpenTelemetry for metrics and logs and OTEL collectors are a few examples. Tools that adopt these open source concepts will be better placed in taking advantage of the benefits of these industry standards.

Custom protocols and proprietary implementations need to be carefully analyzed for the cost versus long-term benefits. For a large organization with diverse technology stacks, we recommend tools that are more aligned with these industry standards rather than going for proprietary solutions. Large organizations may have multiple teams working in different time zones and shifts to resolve a major issue. With standards in place, all teams follow the same methods and it's easier to manage the troubleshooting issues. Teams can gain deeper insights into the behavior of the system using standards as they contain recommended patterns and metrics that should be monitored for a particular system or technology.

Now that you have a general idea about observability tools, the next logical step is to start looking for observability tool prospects for your organization. There are primarily three approaches to choosing the tools, as discussed in the next section.

Build, leverage, or buy?

It's a daunting task to choose the right observability toolset for your organization. Almost every vendor in the analytics and monitoring space has an observability offering. All organizations are often presented with three choices when it comes to selecting a tool:

- Build a tool
- Leverage existing tools
- Buy an off-the-shelf enterprise product

The deciding factors for selection should be observability requirements, risk appetite, investment, and organizational culture.

The **build** strategy is all about developing a solution within the organization with the components available in the public domain, likely using open source tools. It does not necessarily mean developing a tool from scratch, and we don't recommend that either, due to the significant efforts required to make it work in an enterprise environment. Organizations choose to build tools for several reasons:

- First, solutions available on the market may not fully meet the needs of the organization. Building a custom solution using open source technologies allows fine-tuning and customization so that the tool fits the specific requirements of the organization.

- Second, building a custom solution allows better integration with existing systems and infrastructure, resulting in a more seamless and efficient overall system. This is because the internal teams of the organizations know how a particular tool or application is being used.

- Finally, building a custom tool can also lead to cost savings in the long run as the organization will not have to pay for expensive commercial solutions or subscription fees.

With the advent of open source projects and thriving open source communities, this method has been very popular recently for the obvious reason of cost. All open source projects need to be adapted to your organization's requirements, which may require additional development and testing. Hence this strategy is suitable for an organization with a *create* culture, described in *Chapter 6*, where the organization experiments with and innovates new ideas and accepts the risk associated with it. The strategy's greatest disadvantage is that the quantity and quality of technical resources required to build, support, and maintain open-source-based or in-house-developed solutions are quite high. Mismanagement of product development and implementation in the organization can be very costly. Some of the characteristics of the build strategy are summarized here:

- **Agility**: Some organizations prioritize flexibility over effort and risk. Open-source-based custom solutions provide developers and engineers with the flexibility and agility required for solving problems in many ways, making this option suitable for highly automated and integrated environments.

- **Low capital expenditure**: Open source tools are developed, maintained, and supported by individuals in open source communities and hence are practically free, which is very attractive for organizations who want to avoid large capital expenditure in acquiring a tool. Solutions based on these open source tools will only incur adaption and integration costs, which can be minimal compared to the large acquisition cost required for the enterprise's third-party tools.

- **No vendor lock-in**: By relying on a community-driven project, the organization can avoid vendor dependencies, which will provide more flexibility in its operations.

- **Industry-leading solutions**: Since open source projects are at the forefront of innovation and in developing industry standards, organizations can benefit from cutting-edge technologies and attain first-mover advantage in the industry.

- **High risk**: As described previously, adopting an open-source-based solution exposes the organization to the risks related to a lack of formal professional product support, dependency on highly motivated and technical resources, and the technology churn of open source projects.

Now let's look at the **leverage** strategy. Observability tools are supposed to provide a shared view of the system, allowing development, operations, and IT teams to work together more effectively. Sometimes, you might have existing tools or capabilities in your technology ecosystems that can provide the same outcome with minimal effort. This is particularly true in the case of the cloud, where almost all the cloud infrastructure providers (AWS, GCP, Azure, etc.) have these capabilities as part of their offering. If the majority of your applications and services are hosted by any of these cloud service providers, assessing the offering provided by the same vendor is highly advisable. In such cases, an organization can build the observability solution on top of these existing tools/capabilities, by using the resources available in your organization, as they are familiar with the cloud service provider technology landscape and the capabilities and solutions it offers. While leveraging the existing toolset, the following characteristics need to be considered:

- **Cost savings**: Leveraging existing tools can help organizations save on the cost of purchasing and implementing new tools. This can be especially beneficial for cost-sensitive organizations.

- **Familiarity**: Organizations that already have existing tools and technology ecosystems in place are likely to be familiar with how to use them, which can make it easier to get started and get results quickly.

- **Easy integrations**: Existing tools or tools within the current ecosystem may already be integrated with other systems and applications, which can save time and effort in setting up new integrations.

- **Data consistency**: Leveraging existing tools can help organizations maintain consistency in the data they collect and analyze. This can be especially important when working with large or complex datasets.

- **Support and maintenance**: Organizations that leverage existing tools will likely have access to existing commercial and maintenance agreements and technical resources, which can help ensure that the tools continue to function properly and are kept up to date.

- **Risk management**: Leveraging existing tools can help organizations mitigate the risks associated with implementing new tools, such as compatibility issues or data loss.

- **Lack of maturity**: Existing tools may not have been acquired with observability in mind. Hence these tools may not have all the features and capabilities required for a good observability tool. This may result in non-optimal observability solutions.

Buying a purpose-built observability tool requires the least effort, as the vendor already has worked with many technology stacks to provide a tested, validated, and scalable solution. These products are supported by a support agreement, which provides an additional safety net for the organizations that are using these tools. Some of the characteristics of the **buy** strategy are as follows:

- **Professional support**: An off-the-shelf purchase of a tool comes with a support agreement that will take the support and maintenance hassle away from the organization and free up the time and resources to concentrate on using the tool and realizing its value. Also, the vendor will provide patches, new features, and capabilities at regular intervals, based on their product roadmap.

- **Ready to use**: Commercial tools are always tested and validated with various technology stacks and hence can work seamlessly with the targeted technologies. Also, these tools can provide off-the-shelf built-in dashboards and alerts, which help the organization to derive the value quite quickly.

- **Training and documentation**: Generally, all vendor-provided commercial software comes with extensive documentation and well-designed training programs. Organizations can easily tap into these resources and can quickly train engineers and developers in using these tools with ease.

- **High cost**: Commercial off-the-shelf software can be quite expensive to acquire and incur yearly support and licensing costs. Organizations have to take particular care in understanding the license model of any tool and its cost implications.

- **Dependency**: Organizations using commercial software are dependent on the product roadmaps of the vendor. These product roadmaps, technology priorities, and business practices of the vendor may not always align with the organization's requirements and goals.

The decision to buy, leverage, or build observability tools depends on the specific needs, resources, and type of an organization:

- **Build**: Organizations should consider building observability tools if they have the necessary expertise and resources to do so. The build strategy can provide you with a highly flexible, purpose-built, and cost-effective solution if you are comfortable with the risk associated with it.

- **Leverage**: Organizations should consider leveraging existing observability tools if they have existing tools in place that can be used for observability. This can be a cost-effective option for organizations that want to make the most of their existing tools and resources. However, the solution may not be feature-rich, which can result in sub-optimal observability implementation.

- **Buy**: Organizations should consider buying observability tools if they need a fully supported, ready-made solution that can be implemented quickly. But please be mindful of the cost of acquisition and support and resulting vendor dependency.

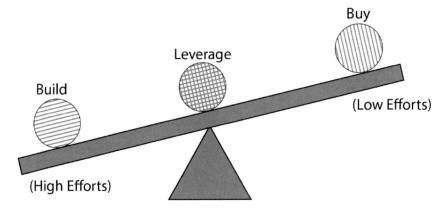

Figure 9.1: See saw balance between build, buy, and leverage

It is important to evaluate the costs, benefits, and risks associated with each option before making a decision. Within your organization, discuss with technical teams and the business to weigh up the pros and cons of each approach and make an informed decision.

This section talked about the desirable features of observability tools that you can use as guardrails to drive discussions and make the right decision for your organization. Since this book intends to help you plan observability for enterprise success, we'll discuss some observability tools in the next section.

Exploring observability tools

Now that we are approaching the end of this book, we believe it would be beneficial to cover some tools and technology references for the different types of monitoring we discussed. From industry experience and exposure, we have curated a list of tools (in no particular order) for infrastructure, application, and business service monitoring, and for managing alerts and incidents. We don't profess to be experts in these tools, so please take these comments as our opinions. We strongly advise you to analyze these tools yourself, based on your requirements and desirable features that we have discussed earlier in the chapter. Also, please keep in mind that you may need more than one tool to meet your requirement; however, please do limit your choices as much as possible for cost optimization and reducing operational overhead. Let's dive right in:

- **Dynatrace, New Relic, and AppDynamics**: Broadly classified as **Application Performance Management (APM)** tools, these are used to provide insights into the performance of applications at the code level. They also provide a good view of the infrastructure and application layer and tracing capabilities for modern applications. Recently, some of these tools have launched into log analytics capability and event correlation as well.

- **Splunk**: Splunk pioneered log analytics and is used to monitor, troubleshoot, and secure infrastructure and applications. Over the last decade, Splunk has expanded its product portfolio to include SIEM solutions, security orchestration and automation tools, and recently APM tools, primarily targeting cloud applications. Splunk can easily ingest data from multiple sources, locations, and infrastructure providers to provide a single pane of glass. This also makes it a good tool for business application monitoring. If your organization operates technology stacks hosted simultaneously in on-premises data centers and also has a multi-cloud strategy, Splunk can be a strong choice.

- **Elasticsearch, Logstash, and Kibana (ELK)**: Built on top of open source projects, ELK is used to analyze log data and monitor infrastructure. It provides a scalable and easy-to-use solution for collecting, processing, and visualizing large volumes of log and event data in real time.

- **AWS Cloudwatch, X-Ray, and OpenSearch**: This is Amazon's observability and monitoring tool stack for log analytics, tracing, application performance, and so on. These tools are fully managed by AWS and cover the full AWS stack. The outcome of the observability tools can be fully integrated with the AWS automation stack, providing seamless automation and workload management capability. It's a good choice to consider if your technology stack is hosted predominantly in AWS.

- **Google Cloud Operations Suite**: This is GCP's observability and monitoring offering, providing capabilities such as APM, log analytics, infrastructure monitoring. Fully managed by GCP, the offering can scale and is well integrated with all the GCP workloads and can easily integrate with GCP automation tools. The solution includes Cloud Logging for data collection, Cloud Monitoring for metric dashboards, and Error Reporting to aggregate and display errors. Additionally, Cloud Trace provides performance insights, Cloud Profiler gathers resource data, and Cloud Debugger inspects running applications in real time without stopping or slowing them down. It's highly advisable for an organization that predominantly has GCP workloads.

- **Zabbix**: Zabbix is an open source monitoring tool that provides the monitoring of various IT components such as servers, applications, network devices, and cloud resources. It supports a wide range of data collection methods, including SNMP, JMX, IPMI, and agents, and it also provides flexible notification mechanisms. Zabbix can scale to large environments and offers high-availability options for enterprise deployments.

- **DataDog**: This is a SaaS-based, AI-enabled monitoring and analytics platform that supports cloud monitoring and security for applications and microservices hosted in the cloud. It can analyze performance data and generate alerts. Along with infrastructure monitoring and APM, it also provides network monitoring, making it a good choice for business application monitoring as well. It is widely used for applications hosted in the cloud.

- **Prometheus**: This is an open source monitoring tool, predominantly for matrices, that can be used to collect and analyze metrics at scale, especially from highly distributed applications and microservices. It is reliable, easy to set up and maintain, and it can easily co-exist with other services in the cloud-native ecosystem, thus gaining popularity.

- **Jaeger and Zipkin**: Both of these are open source distributed tracing systems that allow you to collect and analyze traces from your applications. Jaeger, being more recent, provides support for OpenTracing as well. These tools do not provide a complete observability solution but have a very strong place in the market for distributed tracing.

- **ServiceNow**: A SaaS-based IT service management platform that provides **IT Service Management (ITSM)**, **IT Operations Management (ITOM)**, and **IT Business Management (ITBM)** solutions. It provides a unified platform to manage IT services, incidents, problems, changes, and CMDB, enabling IT teams to streamline their processes and prioritize work based on business needs. Recently, ServiceNow has ventured into the monitoring and log analytics space; however, this capability has not yet reached the maturity level required for enterprise implementation. Still, it continues to be an excellent tool for maintaining CMDB, as discussed in more detail in *Chapter 2*.

- **PagerDuty**: This is a SaaS-based incident management platform that provides a centralized platform for teams to manage and respond to IT infrastructure incidents. The platform integrates with monitoring, alerting, and ticketing systems to provide a comprehensive view of an organization's IT operations.

If your organization already has one or more of these tools but they are being used for a few specific functions, that is perfectly fine too. You can think about how better to adopt the tool by working with the executives and architecture forum. Also, keep in mind that some tools charge separately for some sophisticated features. So, a lot of organizations buy basic versions of a tool and expand as per their business needs. Also, the tools listed previously invest heavily in innovation and future roadmaps. So, always refer to the product documentation online to learn about the latest features.

Emerging observability trends

Observability has been touted as an effective tool for next-generation monitoring. It is being sold as an enhancement from the traditional siloed and vendor-based monitoring to a more coherent and consolidated monitoring solution. With the advent of microservice and cloud-based application architecture, there has been a shift in the IT infrastructure landscape, because of which observability has evolved into a new architecture framework that has influenced the way applications and services are designed and implemented. This evolution will continue in the coming years. The following sections cover a few trends in observability that you need to be aware of and consider while defining observability strategies and tool selection.

Standardizing observability for open source projects

The open source projects and communities that have pioneered observability in its early stages have been actively working for a standardized observability landscape. As we have discussed in the previous chapters, since large organizations use software systems from multiple vendors that follow their own development methodologies and logging standards, engineers will end up using a multitude of tools that are specifically built for these systems. Since the success of observability depends on bringing data from these multiple systems, standardizing the generation and collection of data and data formats makes a world of difference. Open source standards such as OpenTelemetry has been in existence for a while now and are likely to be adopted as a standard by the technology and industry governing bodies such as IELT for internet protocols and communication. OpenTelemetry logs are still being developed and should be mature in a few years. Adoption of these standards by developers and vendors will result in the creation of applications and services that can provide end-to-end and top-to-bottom observability.

Another major development from the open source community is open source tools, which are vendor-agnostic and easily work with open source standards. Tools such as the OTEL collector provide a vendor-agnostic tool to accept, export, share, and process telemetry data at scale. At the time of writing, open source communities are busy with multiple observability projects and initiatives. We expect various projects and initiatives to be consolidated or converged into a few standards and tools. Also, these resulting standards and tools may get recognition from various governing bodies, which will encourage the vendors to adopt these as part of their technology and product roadmap. This will further accelerate the journey to a more unified observability.

Increased adoption of tracing

At the time of writing, tracing is the least used among the three pillars of observability (logs, metrics, and traces, as discussed in detail in *Chapter 2*). Many organizations have not explored the full potential of this yet. Distributed tracing is all about providing context to every activity in an IT system. As more and more workloads become cloud-native, organizations will endorse and implement distributed tracing in a widespread manner. This will result in extending the tracing so that it can be used in a wide range of use cases other than the traditional monitoring of customer experience, business and process optimization, fintech, resource utilization and planning, regulatory compliance, and more. Also, as discussed previously in the *Standardizing observability for open source projects* section, when the open source observability tools and standards mature over the next few years, organizations will find it easier to implement tracing at a larger scale. Hence, organizations should consider these increased adoptions and the resulting data volume, data diversity, and more while considering an observability strategy and the tools to achieve it.

Enhancing security with observability

In the past few years, the sophistication of cybersecurity threats has increased. Criminals and hackers have been very innovative in disrupting IT services across the globe. Increased adoption of cloud technologies and cloud-native applications has made this sophistication more potent. Hence, security professionals are looking for new ways to increase the visibility of how applications and services are designed, developed, run, and consumed in depth, to protect them from cyber threats. Observability is all about collecting and processing data, which shows the state of an application or a service. The same observability data can also tell us about the security vulnerabilities of the application. Hence, using observability tools and data for cyber security use cases is bound to increase in the coming years. The common use cases in demand now are related to Kubernetes and container platforms. However, it has a wide range of applications in app security and code-level security, intrusion detection, and network traffic analysis. As discussed in *Chapter 4*, when we mentioned reusing the data as much as possible, security is another vast paradigm, where the observability data that's collected for IT monitoring can be reused and expand the value proposition. In coming years, we could see the security operations of organizations taking more and more interest in IT observability as a potential data source for augmenting security capabilities.

Auto-healing

As we discussed in *Chapter 1* under the *Benefits of observability* section, auto-healing or self-healing is an emerging area that enables organizations to offer resilient IT services. **Infrastructure as Code** provides the ability for developers and engineers to automate the building and provisioning of infrastructure, using CI/CD tools such as Chef, Puppet, Terraform, and Codefresh. By combining observability and CI/CD tools, developers can fully automate responses that are required for restoring services using CI/CD workflows and use observability tools to trigger the healing process. The healing process can vary from destroying and creating new workloads to scaling infrastructure up or down based on demand, applying configuration changes in response to an IT event in an ITOps context to automated responses to phishing attacks, blocking IPs in firewalls, and isolating suspicious users in a SecOps context. We believe this convergence will continue to evolve and mature in the coming years.

Considering the total cost of ownership for observability

Like any new technology, organizations motivated by the benefits of the new technology will drive the adoption of observability across the organization. Sooner or later, the business realities will kick in and the cost will become questionable. How much is the observability worth? What is the total cost of implementing across organizations and what is the dollar value of these benefits?

As organizations are now in the early stages of implementing observability, in the next few years, these questions will be louder and asked more frequently. We believe that there is no simple answer to these questions. Those organizations that have strived to reduce and consolidate the number of tools, streamline the process or the adoption of observability, and make it easier for people to use will see a reduced **total cost of ownership** (**TCO**) as the consolidation and decommissioning of existing tools can save them license and operational costs. The use of standard collectors across the organization will further reduce the costs related to collecting, transporting, and processing the data. Also, observability is expected to increase the accuracy and reliability of the data and thereby drive operational and business efficiency. Combined, these savings can pay for the observability implementation. Organizations that have failed to drive value from all the aforementioned aspects will be eventually forced to scale back or optimize the scope of the observability implementation to a very few select use cases due to cost pressures. These constrained observability implementation will never be able to reach their full potential and will eventually end up as glorified monitoring tools.

A good example of such a scenario is what happened with big data, the wonder technology pioneered by tech giants such as Google, Facebook, and Apple, which can crunch data at scale and extract value out of a large volume of data. Almost all Fortune 500 companies had a crack at it, but only a few companies became successful in implementing it to its full potential. Hence, it is advisable to keep the TCO question and cost recovery in mind while planning for implementing observability.

Summary

Apart from the theoretical aspects of a technology, concept, or tool, its ultimate success will depend on how it's been implemented and how it is primed to face the present and future challenges of an organization. Hence, while selecting an observability tool or tools, we highly recommend that you concentrate on the practical considerations that the engineers, developers, and business face day to day. Practical considerations such as the types of problems the organization is trying to resolve now and into the future, the skill levels of the consumers, ease of use, operational consideration, the ability to absorb future trends, and more should be given primary consideration compared to considerations such as vendor and technology preferences, past success, product familiarity, and others.

Finally, it is important to account for cost because it is impossible to have access to unlimited resources or unlimited time. Whether the organization chooses to build, leverage, or buy, the money spent must be justified or recovered in some shape or form. It will be hard to recover the cost using a single method, so the organization must employ multiple methods such as cost saving, cost avoidance, improved efficiency, and, if possible, improved revenue generation using observability outcomes over multiple years.

With this chapter, we have come to the end of all technical and organization-related concepts important for implementing enterprise observability. In the next chapter, we summarize all the concepts discussed so far in this book in the form of four interesting case studies. We also introduce a step-by-step framework for starting your observability journey.

Part 3 – Use Cases

This part provides ideas on what an observability implementation looks like in the real world and discusses four case studies of fictional companies, which can be used as total or partial inspiration as suits your organization.

This part has the following chapter:

- *Chapter 10, Kickstarting Your Own Observability Journey*

10

Kickstarting Your Own Observability Journey

This chapter gives you some ideas on what observability implementation looks like in the real world. We will take you through four case studies of fictitious companies, which you can use as inspiration totally or in part and adapt to a version that suits your organization. We have tried to cover different industries to give you a wider range of examples. Throughout the following case studies, we will apply the concepts and practices we have explained in the book. Let's get started!

Understanding the observability implementation workflow

Once an organization has decided to implement observability, the rollout must be done in two stages. The first stage is **preparing and planning** the organizational change, and the second stage is the **implementation**.

Preparation – organization-wide change

The first stage of the observability journey is to prepare the organization for the transition, if required. This includes changing the vision, strategy, organization structure, processes, tools, and so on, and, more importantly, preparing the employees of the organization for the disruption as well as the opportunities this transition offers. If your organization requires some changes, we recommend following the steps discussed in the subsequent sections as part of the first stage.

Step 1 – endorse a multiyear program

As we discussed in *Chapter 6*, observability is all about changing the way the organization thinks, organizes itself, and operates. Making a change in organizational culture is always a multiyear program, and the leaders in the organization need to understand and accept this and commit efforts and resources to this program over multiple years. It is advisable to enlist help from an **organizational change management** professional to plan and manage this change.

Step 2 – establish an observability team

As described in *Chapter 8*, the next step is to set up a centralized observability team to lead, advise, facilitate, and act as a consultant to the wider organization to achieve observability. This team will facilitate various steps that need to be taken within the organization, advise senior management and leaders on the program, and provide continuous support to various teams within the organization in matters related to observability.

Step 3 – establish an observability framework, processes, and tools

With the setup of the observability team, the observability engineers and architects should identify stakeholders with skin in the game and liaise with them to establish an observability framework, an associated process, and a unified set of observability tools and standards for the organization. The potential list of these stakeholders and influencers is explained in *Chapter 8*. At a minimum, we recommended liaising with **enterprise architecture** and **enterprise data governance** teams as enterprise architects can play a very important role in institutionalizing the observability framework and principles on how applications are designed and operated. The data governance team should be able to contribute to helping the engineers be aware of safe data handling methods and regulatory implications. The rest of the stakeholders vary from organization to organization and are also based on business drivers for observability.

Step 4 – evangelize observability

Now the organization has endorsed a multiyear program, committed resources, and established a framework, processes, and tools, it's time to go to town on the new vision. For effective implementation of any organizational change, clearly articulating the vision and strategy behind it is very important. This is where the senior leaders need to work with organization change management experts to announce the new vision, communicate the transition roadmap, and evangelize the need and the benefits of observability. We believe this is a major milestone and critical step in the observability journey, as this is a chance for the organization to show how profound this change is, to display the endorsement and commitment from the senior leaders of the organization, and finally, to help reset the priorities for the rest of the organization. This intends to consistently send out a message that, going forward, observability and data generated from observability will be one of the key outcomes of everything that the organization does.

Step 5 – goals and targets

Evangelizing observability across the organization will prepare the organization for the disruption it can cause and consistently provide guidance and direction related to the change. Apart from this, to drive this change effectively, we believe it's also important to set goals for various application and service teams to achieve every year and also for all related engineers and technology leaders. We believe this is where observability maturity comes into play. Most organizations will classify their services and application into different criticality ratings based on how important those services are. Services for which the organization depends on revenue generation and ensuring services to customers will be deemed highly critical and applications that provide a supporting role will be classified as of lower criticality rating.

We believe an ideal set of goals will be to mandate that each application should achieve a certain maturity level every year. For example, an organization-level target can be as follows:

- **Year 1**: All the criticality 1 applications should achieve a maturity level of *defined* and criticality 2 and 3 applications should achieve a maturity level of *managed*

- **Year 2**: Criticality 1 applications should strive to achieve *quantitatively managed*, and criticality 2 and 3 applications should be at the *defined* level

- **Year 3**: The target of criticality 1 applications should be to achieve a maximum maturity level of *optimize*, criticality 2 applications to attain *quantitatively managed*, and criticality 3 applications can remain at the *defined* level

The maturity levels mentioned above have been discussed in detail in *Chapter 7, Achieving and Measuring Observability Success*. This example of a three-year plan can provide a clear roadmap and end goal for each application, to plan and execute for the next three years and also helps set the expectation of the final maturity level the application must attain at a minimum. These targets by criticality level of application or service for each year can be calibrated and laid down based on the incurred cost, resource requirements, and effort required each year, and also in a way to time and/or maximize the **return on investment** (**ROI**) for the program. The following table summarizes this example:

Application/Service Criticality Level	Year 1	Year 2	Year 3
Criticality 1	Defined	Quantitively managed	Optimize
Criticality 2	Managed	Defined	Quantitively managed
Criticality 3	Managed	Defined	Defined

Table 10.1 – Observability maturity matrix targets

We also strongly recommend that these maturity level goals are incorporated as **key performance indicators** (**KPIs**) in the yearly performance plans for every engineer, architect, and people leader to encourage and incentivize the employees to aid in achieving the observability goals.

Step 6 – measuring and reporting

As discussed in *Chapter 7*, the next important component of the multiyear strategy is continuous and consistent measurement and reporting of the maturity level and progress of the observability plan across the organization. This consistent reporting will help senior management, tech leaders, and the application team monitor the progress and help allocate resources in achieving year-by-year targets set by the multiyear plan. The outcomes of these reports can also be used to measure the KPIs set for the yearly performance review plans for the employees. Therefore, we recommend a quarterly, organization-wide report of the maturity level of each application or service to provide an organization snapshot.

Once the organization has laid out the overall strategy, processes, and guardrails, it's up to the organization as a whole, application teams, architects, engineers, and other employees to adopt the transition and operationalize its day-to-day affairs. We will discuss this in the next section.

Implementation – adoption by the organization

Let's look at some of these logical implementation steps that can be followed. Of course, we cannot vouch for whether these ideas have been implemented in a particular organization, but we can verify that a typical observability implementation will have all the following elements:

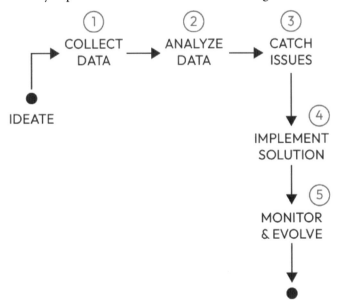

Figure 10.1 – High-level workflow for an observability implementation

The observability team implements all the steps represented in this workflow. They are responsible for facilitating data collection and analysis, help application and support teams in configuring tools for identifying issues, implementing the observability framework, and maintaining it over time. All four case studies you will read about in this chapter have been organized along the same lines.

Let's take a look at the typical activities that will happen in each of the stages in the workflow:

1. **Ideate**:

   A. Identify the gaps in monitoring and understand which challenges are not being covered in the current implementation.

   B. Take stock of the tools and skills available to you that can be used for data collection, analysis, and raising incidents. These tools could be built in-house or purchased from the market.

   C. Engage leadership, support teams, intended users, and technical architects. In other words, they are the stakeholders at this stage.

   D. The deliverable for this stage is a rough plan for your observability implementation with ballpark figures on funding and a placeholder for the tools that will be used.

2. **Collect data**:

   A. Work with application teams to identify all the possible sources of data for the application.

   B. Think through the data collection methods available for each of the data sources. Think of engaging the sourcing team early in this stage if you think that new tools will be required for data collection.

   C. Leverage existing integrations for data collection as much as possible to save time and resources.

   D. Assess whether new integrations are to be built.

   E. Think about the formats in which data is available and assess whether those formats are workable with the available observability tools.

   F. Stakeholders are the centralized observability team and intended users of observability. Enterprise data teams may be optionally involved if any of the data being collected is sensitive.

3. **Analyze the data**:

   A. Apply data literacy to the collected data.

   B. Correlate data from various sources to derive insights into business functions and application services.

   C. Build dashboards for trending and tracking important metrics for the application.

   D. Build KPIs and track them.

   E. Set up policies for data access, encryption, and security.

F. Identify consumers of this data and build interfaces for easy consumption.

G. Like the previous stage, stakeholders at this stage are also the centralized observability team and intended users of observability. It is good to have a clear decision on the target observability maturity level and an observability framework at this stage.

4. **Catch issues**:

A. Set up policies for identifying KPI and **service-level agreement** (**SLA**) breaches.

B. Choose threshold policies for various scenarios – either set static thresholds or adaptive thresholds where the system can learn patterns to call out the outliers.

C. Work with support teams to understand their alerting needs and how they would like to be notified of the issues.

D. Focus on tools that can correlate events and assess the impact on the associated application.

E. Application support teams can either set up the required alerts independently or they can engage the centralized observability team to facilitate the alerts.

5. **Implement solutions**:

A. Implement solutions using automation to save time and cost. This includes self-healing, building deployment pipelines, automating data collection mechanisms, and building solutions for data reliability.

B. Strengthen the process around change management, access controls, data encryption, and data security.

C. The biggest stakeholders at this stage are the centralized observability team and the observability framework. You might need to engage enterprise architects also to influence changes in the areas mentioned in the previous point.

6. **Monitor and evolve**:

A. Keep watch on the observability implementation to see whether the solution can support at least 75% of the incidents.

B. Identify the gaps and add features to enhance the existing solution. It will generally require some work in the second, third, or fourth stage.

C. Periodically review the entire solution (dashboards, alerts, and processes) to keep the solution relevant and useful for the customers. Some other benefits of periodic reviews are early detection of problems, improved efficiency, improved decision-making, increased reliability, compliance, cost savings, and many more.

D. This stage will succeed only with the active participation of users and the centralized observability teams. Leadership needs to facilitate the required traction and funding throughout the journey.

Using the workflow of observability implementation, let's go through the case studies of some fictitious companies where the workflow has been implemented. They are intended to inspire you to apply the workflow to your use case.

> **Important note**
>
> In the context of the subsequent case studies, we are listing here all the benefits of observability that we discussed in *Chapter 1*:
>
> - Correlated applications that deliver higher business value
> - Improved customer experience driving customer loyalty
> - Tools rationalization for improved ROI
> - Focus on not just tech but also the process
> - Data noise is converted into actionable insights
> - Foundation for self-healing architecture
>
> After each case study, we recommend returning to these benefits and determining whether they can be realized. If you think reaping some of these benefits will require more work, think of what you would do differently in your organization to achieve them.

Case study 1 – goFast

In recent times, microservices have knocked out traditional monitoring techniques. So, the first case study focuses on monitoring a microservice-based application in a cloud environment and making them observable.

goFast is a taxi service that has a complex architecture with multiple microservices, each running in its own container, deployed on a cloud platform such as AWS. Various teams at goFast work in collaboration to achieve a single goal – providing the best service to the customer. The tasks of different teams are interwoven, so they focus on teamwork, loyalty, consensus, and frameworks, which allows them to move aggressively through their timelines. Each of these microservices performs a specific function and some of them, when combined, form a business service. For example, one microservice facilitates user logins, another microservice shows available cabs, a third microservice calculates and displays fares, a fourth microservice is invoked in cancellation scenarios, and some microservices handle payments. There are also less complicated microservices such as feedback and advertisement.

Identifying the problem

At goFast, the web of infrastructure is complicated. Their business depends on customer experience and any downtime is harmful to them, because they are a customer-facing app. Monitoring individual microservices is easily possible, but the problem is stitching all the microservices together to see some meaningful application. goFast has a large user base of 2,500 users per minute who are trying to log in, make a booking, cancel a booking, make payments, and much more. All these are the features of the application that a customer can avail. To support this user base, goFast has a huge infrastructure that generates its own data, and the applications running on this infrastructure also generate high-velocity, high-volume data capturing every customer interaction. Typical challenges faced by various engineering and support teams at goFast are as follows:

- **Scalability**: The ability to handle increasing passengers and drivers as their business grows
- **Real-time dispatch**: Ensuring accurate and efficient dispatch of taxis to passengers, with real-time updates on availability and location
- **Payment processing**: Securely processing passenger payments, including integration with multiple payment gateways
- **Route optimization**: Optimizing the routes taken by taxis to minimize time and distance and improve driver efficiency and customer satisfaction
- **Location-based services**: Providing accurate and up-to-date information on driver and vehicle location and estimated arrival times to their customers
- **Vehicle tracking**: Monitoring the real-time location, speed, and condition of vehicles and ensuring passenger safety
- **Data management**: Storing and managing large amounts of customer and transaction data while ensuring data privacy and security
- **Mobile optimization**: Ensuring the app is optimized for mobile devices, with a user-friendly interface and smooth navigation

In the next section, let's look at how these challenges can be addressed.

Addressing the problem

As described in the previous chapters, the first step is to analyze the organization, its culture, its products and services, and the technology stack. Once the strategy, tools, and framework are in place, the developers and operational engineers at goFast can start the implementation. All these services that the customers use at goFast are business functions and are made up of one or more microservices. In traditional monitoring, the goFast monitoring team would have focused only on login failures and set up alerts when failures crossed a particular threshold. In the observability world, the goFast Observability team has configured its observability tools to understand the failure patterns on their own over a given time and classify them as user or application failures. When a user enters an incorrect password, it's a user failure, but when the password validation service is unavailable, it's an application failure. With monitoring, goFast could identify the number of bookings being made per area, but after implementing observability they are also able to identify the areas where bookings are mostly denied by the drivers (a remote area of the city where chances of getting a return passenger are difficult) or the areas where customers often cancel the bookings (a local taxi stand is nearby with economical rates). This data has helped their business team to come up with investment-related plans in these areas.

To set up observability, the goFast observability team started by **identifying the microservices** and their interactions that need to be monitored, which they also term as mapping all possible customer journeys. For example, opening the app, browsing the taxis, and making an advance booking are all examples of a customer journey. These journeys involve the microservices for login, showing available taxis and estimated fares, recording the booking, and sending an appropriate booking confirmation.

Let's review the observability journey at goFast in the context of the observability implementation workflow discussed earlier in this chapter:

- **Ideate**: goFast already had a mature monitoring practice, so they started with evaluating whether they needed observability. All the stakeholders worked together, and they reached a common consensus that the coverage of the IT assets and the correlation between data from different sources could be improved as the **mean time to respond** (MTTR) for incidents was not within acceptable limits. Even if they continued enhancing the monitoring rather than implementing observability, they would not have achieved the desired outcome. So, they organized the available resources – tools and skill sets. For better adoption of observability and to align with their organization's strategy, they discussed with the executives and secured their buy-in. They moved a step ahead, identified the observability implementation users, and discussed their expectations of the solution with them.

> **Important note**
> As discussed in multiple chapters in this book, executives play a major role in implementing good quality observability.

- **Collect data**: Being a taxi service, goFast has contrasting peak loads on different days and at different times of the day, so they are hosted on containers and cloud platforms to manage loads. So, the observability team had to think of appropriate technologies to collect data from Kubernetes and AWS CloudWatch. Cloud teams at goFast volunteered to help the observability team to build a repeatable framework for data collection in a shared responsibility model. The data was in the form of logs, performance metrics, and traces and was collected from the infrastructure, application, and business service layers. Existing data collection integrations were leveraged wherever possible. After reviewing the applications for collecting **application performance management** (**APM**) data, they had to **collaborate** with application engineering teams to instrument the applications to produce the data required for achieving the desired observability. They chose the Prometheus and Dynatrace tools for data collection (refer to *Chapter 9*, the *Exploring observability tools* section, for more references to tool names for data collection). The observability team focused on collecting data for all components of all customer journeys for complete coverage.

- **Analyze data**: The observability team at goFast built several suitable dashboards for tracking and trending relevant metrics and KPIs. Using these dashboards, they can correlate data from multiple microservices to get a view of application services and business functions. At goFast, response times of customer-facing microservices are the most critical metric to be observed. At peak commute hours, the response time might go up by a few milliseconds, and the system should learn that pattern on its own using artificial intelligence. Payments are another key microservice that should always perform within the SLA to minimize customer churn. The observability team also liaised with the developers to change the code to produce a particular missing metric such as `NTP offset` that was critical for collating payments. They chose Splunk for log analysis and visualization to identify patterns and trends in the data and understand the behavior of their microservices (refer to *Chapter 9*, the *Exploring observability tools* section, for more references on tools).

- **Catch issues**: Extensive data collection, data correlation, and analysis enabled the observability team at goFast to identify any issues such as data consistency issues, known errors, performance bottlenecks, inter-service communication errors, or service outages. This helped in achieving their common collaborative goal – excellent customer experience at all times. A dip in response times may be caused by underlying infrastructure or a slow response from a connected microservice. Since they were collecting data for all the microservices, they were able to narrow down the issue very quickly, thus reducing the MTTR. They could also set up incidents and alerts for known issues to quickly resolve issues and implement automation and self-healing wherever possible. With the help of observability tools, the team constantly kept a tab on the agreed SLA for the services and flagged breaches to the teams responsible for maintaining them. The breach thresholds were agreed upon with the support teams during the ideation stage. Since microservices are highly interrelated, their observability team chose tools for incident management that could correlate events from multiple services and quickly generate a list of impacted applications.

- **Implement solutions**: Based on the analysis, the application engineering teams implemented solutions to address any identified issues, such as increasing the number of replicas of a microservice to handle the increased load or adding load balancers to evenly distribute traffic. Improvising the **Information Technology Infrastructure Library** (ITIL) process and sanitizing the development team's logging practices were also part of the implementation.

- **Monitor and evolve**: The observability team at goFast continuously monitored the application and its microservices to ensure that the solutions implemented were effective and that any new issues were being identified and addressed promptly. Implementation was repeatedly reviewed, and any scenarios in the existing dashboards, alerts, machine learning capabilities, and automated workflows that may have been missed were included. The team also increased focus on automation and improving the process at every iteration (recall from *Chapter 5* that dashboards and alerts need to be periodically reviewed to keep them relevant). This led to the development of monitoring frameworks at goFast, which included best practices for monitoring certain types of application components.

This use case demonstrates how observability can be used to gain insights into the behavior and performance of a complex, distributed system and how it can be used to identify and resolve issues promptly.

Consider whether goFast will be able to realize the benefits of observability (listed earlier) based on the case study we just discussed. If you think that reaping some benefits will require more work, think of what you would do differently in your organization to achieve them.

Case study 2 – superEats

Next, we bring you a case study of observability in the food industry for a food manufacturing company named superEats. They have an end-to-end supply chain starting with procuring the produce from farmers and fisheries processing the food, and delivering it to retailers and wholesalers for sale. There are multiple moving parts at superEats, so the only way for them to work like a well-oiled machine is to have a rounded organizational structure and processes. They have a control culture that keeps the moving parts in check but it also resists change. But the team at superEats was inspired by the benefits of observability and wanted to implement it. Their journey is discussed in the following subsections.

Identifying the problem

The company produces and distributes a variety of food products and needs to ensure that they are safe to consume and of high quality at all times. The supply chain at superEats is shown in the following diagram:

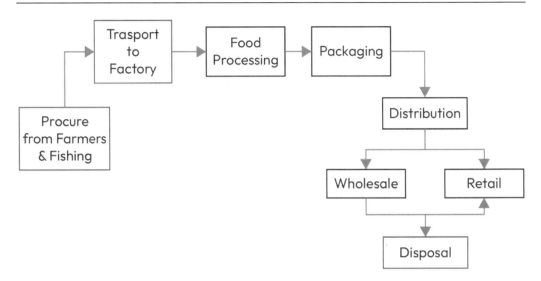

Figure 10.2 – Supply chain at superEats

In their day-to-day operations, they face the following challenges:

- Ensuring that the food products are safe for consumption, meeting regulatory standards, and preventing foodborne illnesses

- Managing the procurement of raw materials and the production and distribution of finished products

- Maintaining the quality of products, ensuring consistency in taste, appearance, and safety

- Balancing the cost of production with profitability and competitiveness in the market

- Implementing environmentally friendly practices and reducing waste in the manufacturing process

- Developing new products to meet changing consumer preferences and stay ahead of competitors

- Developing attractive and informative packaging that meets legal requirements and enhances product appeal

It's clear that superEats has a lot of moving parts, many of which work in tandem. Let's look at how they can be managed efficiently.

Addressing the problem

In this section, let's review the observability journey at superEats in the context of the observability implementation workflow discussed earlier in this chapter. Keep in mind that as per the culture of their organization, they resist change, and so you will find them taking very small, definitive steps:

- **Ideate**: The observability journey started with identifying the different stages of the supply chain at superEats that need to be monitored, such as the sourcing of raw materials, production, packaging, and distribution. All other activities such as engaging leadership, engineering, and support teams, as discussed in the typical activities in the ideate stage in the *Understanding the observability implementation workflow* section of this chapter, were followed.

- **Collect data**: Data gathering was set up from various sources such as temperature sensors, humidity sensors, and **radio-frequency identification** (**RFID**) tags to track the movement of products through the supply chain. superEats involves more firmware than software; the data collected was still in the form of logs and metrics from firmware and the form of logs, metrics, and traces from the software components. There was also hardware and software involved at some stages such as distribution systems, payment collection, and others that will generate data as per traditional IT infrastructure. Here, OpenTelemetry was highly useful in collecting time-series-based data from firmware. The following figure represents the sources and formats of the data available at superEats:

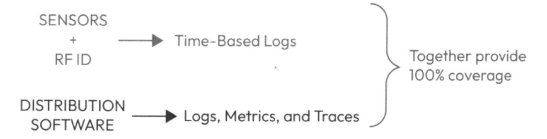

Figure 10.3 – Data sources and formats at superEats

After reviewing the data sources and formats, the observability team assessed whether their tools could receive and process data from a mix of firmware and software sources. They finally ended up investing in some new tools for their requirement. This took a long time, as incorporating a new tool is a huge change, and the team took measurable steps before integrating the tool with existing sources.

- **Analyze data**: Once data collection was successful, superEats achieved an end-to-end view of their supply chain as they could perfectly build a chronological timeline of events by combining the data from the firmware and software. It helped in identifying the strong and faulty sections of the supply chain. Furthermore, they configured their observability tools to build dashboards to identify patterns and trends in the data and understand the behavior of the supply chain. Because of the nature of the data, engineers at superEats had to apply data literacy, especially for the data coming from firmware, to derive meaningful insights from it. They engaged technical teams from firmware providers for this. With 100% coverage of their supply chain, they could also build dashboards around important KPIs such as lead time, order fulfillment rate, carrier performance, supplier performance, and many more. Since the data at superEats involved sensitive data in the packaging and distribution stages, they also devised policies for data access, encryption, and security.

- **Catch issues**: All the collected data was then used to identify any issues such as temperature deviations that could affect product quality, integration issues, data breaches, or delays in the movement of products through the supply chain. Here, the observability tools chosen by superEats for dashboards, alerts, and incidents were used to inform the application or infrastructure support teams as applicable about further action required on the issue (refer to *Chapter 9* for more information on tool references). This change was seen as a positive outcome and was embraced without much resistance.

- **Implement solutions**: Based on the analysis, solutions were implemented to address any identified issues, such as adjusting the temperature settings in storage facilities or implementing a new logistics system to improve the efficiency of the supply chain. Data enables driving business decisions, and that is why observability is extremely important, as it not only monitors the application but also correlates transactions across applications to get more insights into the business activities. superEats has many moving parts outside and inside their manufacturing plant, so they have invested heavily in driving cultural changes and adopting strict practices around change management for managing and minimizing impact of all major and minor changes.

- **Monitor and evolve**: The supply chain is at the heart of superEats, and it is continuously monitored to ensure that the solutions are effective and contribute to identifying and addressing issues that were not covered earlier. superEats takes food quality very seriously, so they do a more frequent review of observability artifacts around that than other components. It has greatly helped in cost-savings and improved decision-making as their admin teams can tweak distribution accordingly or send out relevant comms to their customers.

We chose this use case to demonstrate how observability can be used to gain insight into the behavior and performance of a complex supply chain and how it can be used to identify and resolve issues related to product quality and efficiency promptly. It also gives you an idea that observability is not limited to software-based applications; it is for any applications that generate data that can be collected. The rest is achievable using observability tools.

Consider whether superEats will be able to realize the benefits of observability listed earlier. If you think that reaping some benefits will require more work, think of what you would do differently in your organization to achieve them.

Case study 3 – bigBuys

Now, let's discuss Observability implementation at an e-commerce platform named bigBuys. It allows users to purchase products online. It has a large user base, and they operate across multiple geographies. bigBuys aggressively focuses on creating and innovating without any restrictions on processes or traditions. They are a start-up and have a creative culture.

We chose this case study as it is a an area that will be familiar to many and is quite relatable. The case study focuses on understanding the performance and behavior of the application, as well as identifying any potential issues that may arise. Remember that with observability, the focus changes from monitoring the known to understanding the application's behavior and the underlying systems.

Identifying the problem

Like all other large-scale e-commerce platforms, bigBuys also has the following challenges in maintaining its website and managing customer satisfaction:

- **Scalability**: The ability to handle an increasing number of users and transactions as the business grows

- **Security**: Protecting sensitive customer information and maintaining the integrity of online transactions

- **Reliability**: Ensuring the website is always available and functioning correctly, with minimal downtime

- **Performance**: Optimizing the website's speed and responsiveness to provide a seamless user experience

- **Integration**: Integrating the website with multiple systems, such as payment gateways, shipping providers, and inventory management systems

- **Personalization**: Providing a personalized experience for each customer, including recommendations, customized content, and dynamic pricing

- **Data management**: Storing and managing large amounts of customer and transaction data, while ensuring data accuracy and accessibility

- **Mobile optimization**: Ensuring the website is optimized for mobile devices that are increasingly used for online shopping

- **Multichannel selling**: Managing sales through multiple channels, including online, in-store, and through marketplaces

How can these challenges be addressed? We'll look at this in the next section.

Addressing the problem

Let's review the observability journey at bigBuys in the context of the observability implementation workflow discussed earlier in this chapter:

- **Ideate**: bigBuy's e-commerce platform allows users to purchase its products online. Keeping the challenges in mind, they wanted to make them more observable. It is a given fact that problems will happen in the application: Ninjas of the monitoring and observability field play around with minimizing the business impact by capturing the issues before they happen or having enough data to identify the root cause of the issues when they occur. The observability team performed a detailed review of the tools and skills available at their disposal for implementing observability and captured the findings in the plan for achieving observability. They had discussions with the relevant teams to gather problem scenarios and ideate on how quickly the issues could be notified using alerts or self-healed wherever applicable.

- **Collect data**: The observability team at bigBuys was facing a lot of challenges and lacked a clear agenda for improving website performance and customer experience, so they started with collecting data from various sources, such as web server logs, to understand the number of requests made to the server and the response time; application logs to understand the behavior of the application and any errors that may have occurred; and performance metrics such as CPU and memory usage to understand the resource utilization of the application and user feedback. While this sounds straightforward in theory, planning for data collection is very time-consuming as it involves data sources on-premises, in the cloud, and in containers. By enabling data collection for all sources, all at once, bigBuys took a huge experimental risk as they did not know the clear benefit of this data at the collection stage. But the culture of their organization allowed them to do it. They could also relatively freely invest in the required tools. As we know, the data can be in the form of logs, metrics, or traces and may come at different velocities from different sources. Also, they had to focus on data storage and processing in the available observability toolset with special attention to data encryption and security policies.

- **Analyze data**: All the data collected in the previous stage was then used to identify trends and track performance over time and to analyze customer behavior, such as purchase history, browsing habits, and feedback, to better understand customer needs and preferences. Data from the web application was used to analyze product sales, performance, and customer feedback to inform product development and marketing strategies. To maintain the desired performance of the website, the team analyzed website traffic data, including source, volume, and demographics, to understand user behavior and improve website design. One of the major aspects of the success of e-commerce platforms is customer satisfaction. So, the observability team kept a watch on data on website performance, including page load time, bounce rate, and conversion rate, to improve the overall user experience. The goal of all the data analysis was to improve customer satisfaction, feedback, ratings, and reviews (refer to *Chapter 9* for ideas on the tools that can be used for data analysis and visualizations). Again, the focus was on long-term growth, and the steps for achieving it were started early as per their creative culture. Along with data analysis, bigBuys set up a strict policy around data access to keep them compliant with in-country rules in all geographies.

- **Catch issues**: bigBuys' IT team constantly faced the following IT issues and was looking for solutions to help them become better at resolving the issues as they occurred:

  - **Slow performance**: The website was slow to load and respond, causing frustration for users and potential loss of sales. It was also unavailable at times

  - **Security breaches**: Unauthorized access to sensitive customer information, including credit card numbers and personal details

  - **Payment processing issues**: Problems with payment processing, such as failed transactions or incorrect billing information

  - **Data loss**: Loss of important customer or transaction data, potentially affecting business operations and customer trust

  - **Technical errors**: Errors in the website code or configuration, causing unexpected behavior or broken links

  - **System failures**: Failure of critical systems, such as payment processing, order management, or inventory management, causing business disruption

  - **Cyber-attacks**: Attempts to hack the website or steal customer data, potentially causing data loss or financial losses

  - **Human error**: Mistakes made by employees or contractors, such as incorrect data entry or misconfigured systems

  - **Third-party issues**: Problems with third-party services, such as payment gateways, shipping providers, or data center outages, causing business disruption

  By collecting data and applying data literacy while analyzing it, bigBuys' IT team could set up sufficient self-healing, incidents, and alerts to notify their support teams of the issues. The observability team started off by talking to the support engineers responsible for managing a particular service about their problems and preferred mode of notifications. bigBuys uses ServiceNow for incident management, which can easily correlate events from various services and helps to quickly assess the impact of the incident. At an organizational level, bigBuys also strengthened its change management processes to minimize human error.

- **Implement solutions**: Based on the insights and learnings from the previous three stages, the observability team advised application engineers to implement solutions around mobile app optimization, payment processing, website security, and deployment pipelines. Although the application support team resolved the incidents, the observability team could tag incidents to a particular category and share their findings with the application teams to work on continual improvement in the areas that showed the maximum number of incidents in a particular category. bigBuys also invested time and resources in data security to ensure their customers can trust them while using their services.

- **Monitor and evolve**: While implementing solutions, the observability team continued to monitor the application to ensure that the solutions implemented were effective and that any new issues were identified and addressed promptly. The periodic observability implementation review helped bigBuys improve website performance, meet compliance requirements, increase security, and benefit from better fraud detection. In the words of an employee from the **customer experience (CX)** team at bigBuys, "*The periodic reviews have helped in the early detection of problems and have prepared our engineering teams to implement a solution for prevention in time or provide guardrails for a quick resolution.*"

Consider whether bigBuys will be able to realize the benefits of observability listed earlier. If you think that reaping some benefits will require more work, think of what you would do differently in your organization to achieve them.

Case study 4 – gruvyCars

The last case study is from the automobile industry of a company named gruvyCars that manufactures connected cars. The goal is to monitor the performance of the pipeline that manufactures connected cars. Connected cars are equipped with various sensors and systems that collect data on the car's performance, and this data can be used to gain insight into the stability of the pipeline and the car's behavior during manufacturing and identify any issues that may arise. gruvyCars needs to remain competitive in the market to maintain its market share, so everything they do is focused on setting aggressive targets and deadlines. Fewer issues in the manufacturing pipeline are directly proportional to faster delivery, so they decided to get started with observability. Clearly, gruvyCars has a competitive culture.

Identifying the problem

At a high level, the following steps are involved in the manufacturing pipeline at gruvyCars:

1. **Concept and design**: During this stage, the engineers develop a concept for the connected car and design the various components and systems used in the vehicle. This stage involves collaboration between various departments, such as engineering, design, and product management. It is also necessary to constantly adapt to changing consumer preferences to remain competitive. This requires significant investment in research and development, as well as changes in manufacturing processes.

2. **Prototyping and testing**: After the design is finalized, prototypes of the connected car are built and tested. This stage is critical for identifying potential design issues and ensuring that the car meets all regulatory and safety requirements.

3. **Component manufacturing**: During this stage, individual components of the connected car are manufactured, such as the engine, transmission, and electrical systems. There is a dependency on a complex network of suppliers and vendors to provide raw materials and components. Any disruption in this supply chain can cause delays and impact production schedules. Moreover, the technology required for automated cars can be expensive, making them more expensive to produce than traditional cars. At each step, gruvyCars needs to find ways to reduce costs while maintaining high levels of quality and safety.

4. **Assembly**: The components are then assembled into complete vehicles. This includes body assembly, chassis assembly, engine and transmission installation, electrical systems installation, and interior assembly. This stage utilizes robots for automated production line processes such as welding, painting, installation, transmission, and more.

5. **Quality control**: Before the connected cars are delivered to customers, they undergo a series of quality control checks to ensure that they meet all specifications and standards. Quality control issues lead to defects, recalls, and other costly problems. Therefore, the team needs checks to ensure a high degree of precision and quality control so that all components fit together seamlessly and that the final product meets safety and performance standards. In addition, it is necessary to comply with a wide range of environmental and regulatory requirements, including emissions standards, safety regulations, and labor laws. Failing to meet any of these requirements can result in fines, legal action, and damage to the company's reputation.

6. **Software integration**: Finally, the software that enables the connected car's various functions is integrated into the vehicle. It is highly complex and must be carefully developed, tested, and integrated with the hardware. This stage may include testing and debugging the software to ensure it functions correctly. In addition, automated cars rely on a range of complex technologies, including sensors, cameras, and computer systems. These technologies must be integrated and tested to ensure that they work seamlessly together. This requires specialized skills and software development expertise, which may differ from the skills needed in traditional car manufacturing.

It is evident that there are a large number of interdependent processes involved. Any bottleneck in the production line can cause delays and reduce efficiency. Identifying and resolving bottlenecks is crucial to maintaining production schedules and controlling costs.

Let's look at how these issues can be handled using observability.

Addressing the problem

Let's review the observability journey at gruvyCars in the context of the workflow discussed earlier in this chapter:

- **Ideate**: The observability team at gruvyCars first identified the systems and sensors that need to be monitored, such as the engine, transmission, and braking systems, as well as the goals of the intended observability implementation. Observability helped in understanding the behavior of the robotic arms that built the cars. With monitoring, they could know the number of cars being manufactured, but with observability, they could know the speed and angles at which the robotic arm operates. They could correlate the speed of one production line with another and identify bottlenecks before they became a problem. The team engaged all relevant parties, such as leadership, support teams, users, and technical architects, in the initial stages of the observability journey. When their leadership team could relate observability benefits with the faster time to market, they gave a clear agenda on the expected outcome and demanded that the observability team move aggressively. They also reviewed their existing centralized monitoring system to assess whether they were well equipped to ingest and process the incoming data. Luckily, they found that their existing tools were underutilized and were capable of handling the expected data volumes, so they saved on the investments in new tools.

- **Collect data**: Data for connected cars was collected from sensors and the telematics devices installed in the firmware, software and robots being used in the manufacturing pipeline to collect and transmit data. The majority of this data was metric-based and was collected easily via OpenTelemetry. Not all tools can receive, process, and store telemetry data. So, they consciously further reviewed the existing toolset to stay aligned with the data sources and formats.

- **Analyze data**: Using the data analysis tools listed in *Chapter 9*, the observability team at gruvyCars analyzed the following using the data collected from connected cars manufacturing pipeline:

  - **Production efficiency**: This measures the productivity of the manufacturing process, including the number of units produced per hour, the average time per unit, and the utilization rate of production equipment.

  - **Quality control**: This measures the number of defects and warranty claims in the manufacturing process, including the defect rate per unit and the number of customer complaints.

  - **Lead time**: This measures the time between the start of the manufacturing process and delivery to the customer, including the time to produce the product, the time to transport the product, and the time to clear customs.

  - **Product traceability**: This measures the ability to track the product from the raw material stage to the end customer, including the use of serial numbers, barcodes, and RFID tags.

  - **Environmental sustainability**: This measures the impact of the manufacturing process on the environment, including the use of renewable energy, the reduction of greenhouse gas emissions, and the use of recycled materials.

They developed dashboards for tracking the key metrics and KPIs for end-to-end visibility of their car manufacturing pipeline and its performance. This end-to-end view could only be created by leveraging the capability of the observability tools to correlate data from various applications and in different formats. gruvyCars' manufacturing pipeline generated time-series-based data in the form of logs and metrics, which helped in deriving business-relevant insights for speed and performance.

- **Catch issues**: With the availability of data and the ability to correlate it, identifying any issues such as engine problems, transmission faults, braking issues, hacking, malware, data breaches, reliability of sensors, communication networks and software, and compatibility and interoperability between different connected car systems and networks all became easier, thus improving development cycles and quality checks. The gruvyCars observability team set up alerts and dashboards on these issues to keep them up to date on the performance of the cars, which helped in resolving issues in the least possible time. They also set up KPIs for each important step in their pipeline, which are constantly monitored to ensure smooth functioning. This has helped improve customer experience, which is the constant focus of gruvyCars as they are a market culture type of organization.

- **Implement solutions**: Based on the analysis, the observability team worked with application engineering and support teams to implement solutions to address any identified issues. Observability gave them the power to correlate data from various systems quickly and in real time. It provided enough data for the support teams to conclude quickly and resolve the problem.

- **Monitor and evolve**: The observability team continuously monitored the performance of the car manufacturing pipeline to ensure that any issues were identified and addressed promptly. The team also kept an eye on the changes required in the observability implementation. In industries such as connected cars, data sources and data formats do not change frequently, but the team still periodically reviewed the relevance of alerts, dashboards, and self-healing workflows. They also reviewed whether any new customer journeys that were recently added were being covered.

Consider whether gruvyCars will be able to realize the benefits of observability listed earlier. If you think that reaping some benefits will require more work, think of what you would do differently in your organization to achieve them.

Summary

These case studies are just examples. The situations you experience might have a different set of data sources and issues depending on the context and complexity of the system that is being studied.

It is time to sign off. We wish you all the best for your observability journey!

Index

Packtpub.com

Subscribe to our online digital library for full access to over 7,000 books and videos, as well as industry leading tools to help you plan your personal development and advance your career. For more information, please visit our website.

Why subscribe?

- Spend less time learning and more time coding with practical eBooks and Videos from over 4,000 industry professionals

- Improve your learning with Skill Plans built especially for you

- Get a free eBook or video every month

- Fully searchable for easy access to vital information

- Copy and paste, print, and bookmark content

Did you know that Packt offers eBook versions of every book published, with PDF and ePub files available? You can upgrade to the eBook version at packtpub.com and as a print book customer, you are entitled to a discount on the eBook copy. Get in touch with us at customercare@packtpub.com for more details.

At www.packtpub.com, you can also read a collection of free technical articles, sign up for a range of free newsletters, and receive exclusive discounts and offers on Packt books and eBooks.

Other Books You May Enjoy

If you enjoyed this book, you may be interested in these other books by Packt:

DevSecOps in Practice with VMware Tanzu

Parth Pandit, Robert Hardt

ISBN: 9781803241340

- Build apps to run as containers using predefined templates
- Generate secure container images from application source code
- Build secure open source backend services container images
- Deploy and manage a Kubernetes-based private container registry
- Manage a multi-cloud deployable Kubernetes platform
- Define a secure path to production for Kubernetes-based applications
- Streamline multi-cloud Kubernetes operations and observability
- Connect containerized apps securely using service mesh

Cloud-Native Observability with OpenTelemetry

Alex Boten

ISBN: 9781801077705

- Understand the core concepts of OpenTelemetry
- Explore concepts in distributed tracing, metrics, and logging
- Discover the APIs and SDKs necessary to instrument an application using OpenTelemetry
- Explore what auto-instrumentation is and how it can help accelerate application instrumentation
- Configure and deploy the OpenTelemetry Collector
- Get to grips with how different open-source backends can be used to analyze telemetry data
- Understand how to correlate telemetry in common scenarios to get to the root cause of a problem

Packt is searching for authors like you

If you're interested in becoming an author for Packt, please visit `authors.packtpub.com` and apply today. We have worked with thousands of developers and tech professionals, just like you, to help them share their insight with the global tech community. You can make a general application, apply for a specific hot topic that we are recruiting an author for, or submit your own idea.

Share Your Thoughts

Now you've finished *Implementing Enterprise Observability for Success*, we'd love to hear your thoughts! Scan the QR code below to go straight to the Amazon review page for this book and share your feedback or leave a review on the site that you purchased it from.

`https://packt.link/r/1-804-61569-2`

Your review is important to us and the tech community and will help us make sure we're delivering excellent quality content.

Download a free PDF copy of this book

Thanks for purchasing this book!

Do you like to read on the go but are unable to carry your print books everywhere?

Is your eBook purchase not compatible with the device of your choice?

Don't worry, now with every Packt book you get a DRM-free PDF version of that book at no cost.

Read anywhere, any place, on any device. Search, copy, and paste code from your favorite technical books directly into your application.

The perks don't stop there, you can get exclusive access to discounts, newsletters, and great free content in your inbox daily

Follow these simple steps to get the benefits:

1. 1. Scan the QR code or visit the link below

https://packt.link/free-ebook/9781804615690

2. 2. Submit your proof of purchase

3. 3. That's it! We'll send your free PDF and other benefits to your email directly

Made in United States
Orlando, FL
04 January 2024

42091040R00093